P9-CCX-011

Yesterday in HAWAI'I

A VOYAGE THROUGH TIME

Yesterday in HAWAI'I

A VOYAGE THROUGH TIME

BY SCOTT C. S. STONE
PICTURE EDITOR: MAZEPPA K. COSTA

ISLAND HERITAGE
PUBLISHING

Dawn.
In the wake of
ancient voyagers,
the contemporary
voyaging canoe
Hōkūle'a approaches

Hawai'i Island as
lava from Kilauea
Volcano's east rift
settles into the sea,
creating new
land, 1991.

For Simon Cardew,
in memoriam

Photo: ©Monte Costa

"A Man of the Sandwich
Islands in a Mask."
Engraving from John
Webber, artist on Captain
James Cook's third voyage.

Copyright ©2003 Island Heritage Publishing
All rights reserved. Except for brief passages quoted in
a review, no part of this book may be reproduced in
any form or by any means, electronic or mechanical,
including photocopying and recording, or by any
information storage and retrieval system, without
permission in writing from the publisher.

Published and distributed by
ISLAND HERITAGE PUBLISHING
ISBN 0-89610-141-X

Address orders and correspondence to:

ISLAND HERITAGE
PUBLISHING
94-411 Kō'aki Street
Waipahu, Hawai'i 96797
For Orders: 800-468-2800
For Information: 808-564-8800
Fax: 808-564-8877
www.islandheritage.com

Printed in China
First edition, Fouth Printing, 2005

DESIGNED BY DANVERS FLETCHER

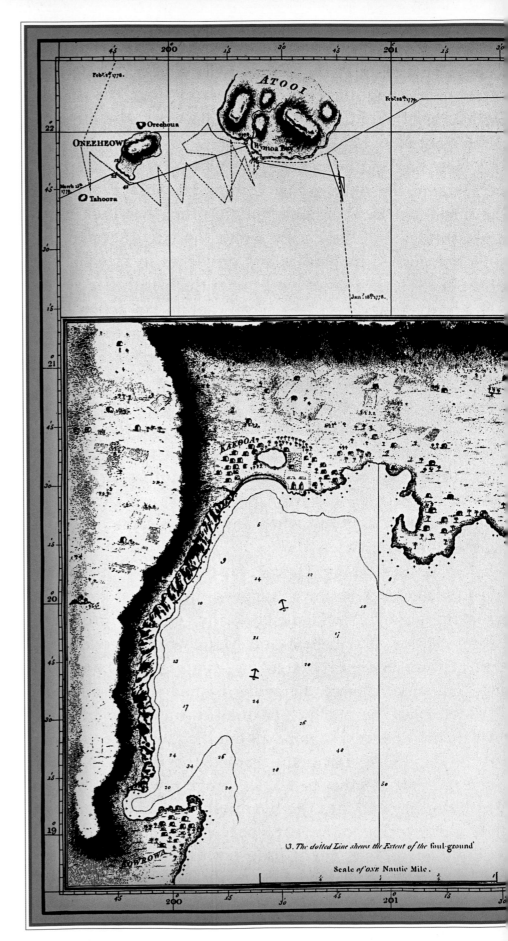

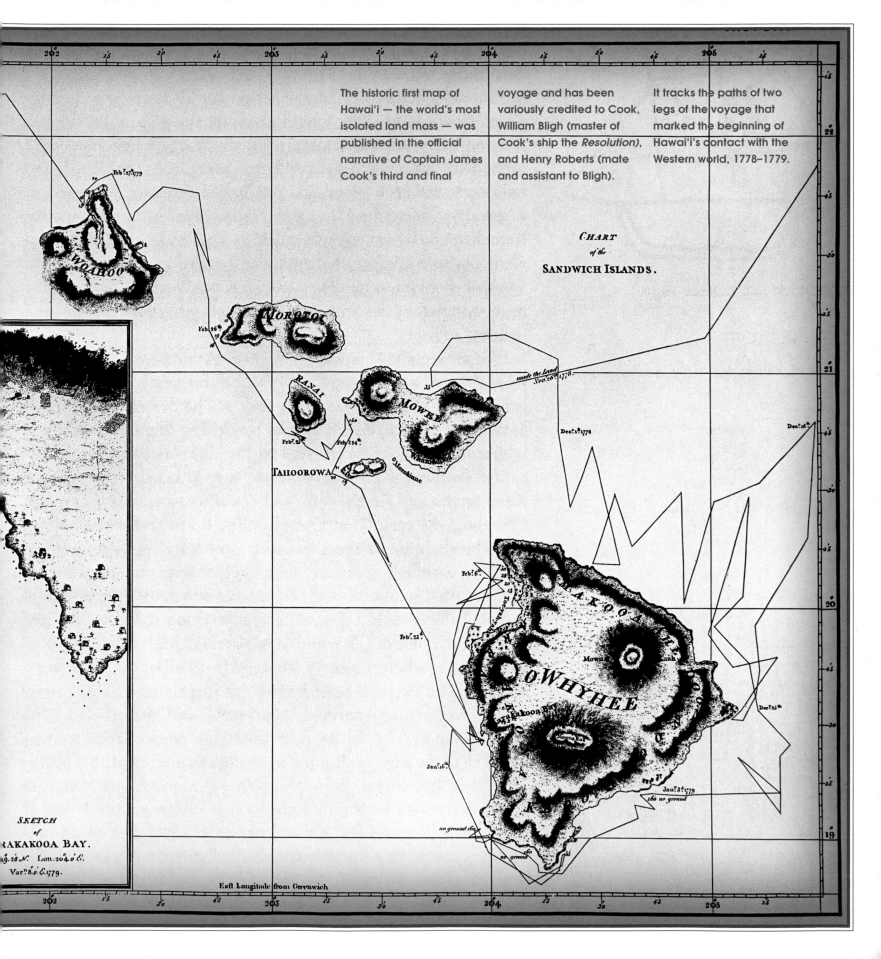

The historic first map of Hawai'i — the world's most isolated land mass — was published in the official narrative of Captain James Cook's third and final voyage and has been variously credited to Cook, William Bligh (master of Cook's ship the *Resolution*), and Henry Roberts (mate and assistant to Bligh). It tracks the paths of two legs of the voyage that marked the beginning of Hawai'i's contact with the Western world, 1778–1779.

CHART
of the
SANDWICH ISLANDS.

WOAHOO

Feb. 27th 1779

MOROTOI

Feb. 26th

RANAI

Feb. 25th

Feb. 24th

MOWEE

WHARRETA

TAHOOROWA

O Morokinne

made the land
Nov. 26th 1778

Dec. 1st 1778

Dec. 1st

Feb. 6th

Feb. 23d

OWHYHEE

Mowna

Karakooa Bay

Jan. 16th

Jan. 3d 1779

160 no ground

no ground 160

no ground

Dec. 25th

East Longitude from Greenwich

SKETCH
of
RAKAKOOA BAY.
...9.28 N. Lon. 204.0 E.
Var. 8.0 E. 1779.

Contents

"La Plage d'Honoloulou a Oahou" (The Beach at Honolulu on Oahu) — interpretation by Auguste Borget of active village life along the shoreline, probably at Waikiki. The drawing suggests the canoe's pivotal role in the lives of Hawaiians, c. 1840s.

A sense of time's footfalls — *lei maile* near the edge of Halemaʻumaʻu fire pit, Kilauea Volcano Crater.

Introduction

The great Polynesian voyages of discovery across the Pacific, beginning with people of the Lapita culture in Southeast Asia some fifteen hundred years before the birth of Christ and culminating in the discovery of the Hawaiian Islands, were arguably the greatest human dispersal in history. What followed was epic in its own way—Hawai'i came out of a profound isolation to become home for people from all over the world, people who fashioned a society in which all were equal regardless of race. It could not have happened everywhere, and it has hardly happened anywhere.

And Hawai'i, which experienced internecine warfare and political upheavals, did not merely survive but prospered in an aura of equality. The edifice that became a society of equal people was not built in a day, nor was it always easy, but in the end people of goodwill were able to be neighbors and business partners and to court future spouses from a variety of other races.

The influx of foreigners filled the Islands with new and sometimes curious ideas—new music and festivals, foods and customs, and ways of looking at things. New gods came as well, and new commerce—new work to occupy the days. Some uniquely Hawaiian concepts were lost in the rush to progress, but more often there was a kind of Hawaiian patina over the new things, so that Hawaiian concepts and styles did not disappear but were shared among the stream of later immigrants. Hawai'i became a society that celebrated its differences as well as its similarities.

Some years, even some decades, were better than others, but that is the nature of time's passage. Hawai'i has known downtimes of economic woes, often because of influences from beyond the reef. Recessions and labor

On voyages of validation, Hawaiians of the 20th and 21st centuries sail in support of the theory that ancient Pacific wayfinders did intentionally navigate over thousands of miles of open ocean, using only traditional navigational methods. Left: Design of the *Hōkūleʻa* is believed to replicate prehistoric Pacific voyaging canoes. In 25 years, beginning with a 5,600-mile round-trip Hawaiʻi/Tahiti voyage, *Hōkūleʻa* navigators successfully traveled 100,000 miles, reaching the three corners of the Polynesian triangle and the West Coast of the United States.

Photo: ©Monte Costa

disputes on the American Mainland have impacted Hawaiʻi. But there have been great times as well, when people of the Islands knew a lifestyle that others could envy. It is notable that in both good times and bad the people of Hawaiʻi have maintained an appreciation for their stunning environment, making even the bad times often seem better than conditions and situations in other places.

Hawaiʻi has developed from a group of chiefdoms into a kingdom, a provisional government, a republic, a territory, and finally a state of the United States. It has known monarchs and pirates, con men and heroes. It is a fragile ecosystem replete with volcanic eruptions, earthquakes, and *tsunami*, yet somehow it is enduring. Its history is as turbulent as it is colorful. As in any society, however, the ordinary people going about the ordinary business of their lives are what make a community and a history, so it is valuable to look back at the people and their activities to get a sense of time's footfalls. The photographs in this book are snapshots of some of the people and events that help illuminate Hawaiʻi's yesterdays.

Chapter 1

At the time when the earth became hot

At the time when the heavens turned about

At the time when the sun was darkened

To cause the moon to shine

The time of the rise of the Pleiades

The slime, this was the source of the earth

The source of the darkness that made darkness

The source of the night that made night

The intense darkness, the deep darkness

Darkness of the sun, darkness of the night

Nothing but night.

—Martha Warren Beckwith, The *Kumulipo*

(Hawaiian genealogical prayer chant)

Below: Louis Choris, artist on Otto von Kotzebue's ship *the Rurick*, 1816, rendered this "Woman of the Sandwich Islands" with dignity befitting the chiefly rank signified by her *lei niho palaoa* — a neckpiece of multilengths of braided human hair hung with a pendant of carved whale's tooth.

Uniformed in masklike gourd helmets topped with foliage and hung with strips of *kapa* (bark cloth), paddlers of a small double-hulled canoe seem to be en route to a ceremonial occasion, accompanied by *kāhuna* (priests), idols, and a sacrificial pig. Engraving after Webber.

The Hawaiians' view of their origins and development is mystical and poetic. It is a view married to a rock-hard pragmatism, for the Polynesians who spread across the Pacific and in time became Hawaiians were a practical people, attuned to the earth and the sea. Their story is not one of passive adaptation but one of interaction with new environments and ecosystems. When they sailed from the Marquesas and Tahiti they brought their sustenance—pigs, yams, taro, bananas, breadfruit—sixteen species of crop plants and animals. When they settled in the land they named Hawai'i, they altered the landscape to suit their needs. They used fire to clear fields, diverted streams to make irrigation systems, and built large fishponds.

By the year 1200 the leeward coasts of the main Islands had permanent settlements. By 1400 the leeward

Above: Hawaiian idols ranged in size from towering temple images to tiny gods under 12 inches. Made variously of wood, stone, sea-urchin spine, and net-covered basketry plugged with feathers, their detail elements included pearl shells, human hair, bones, seeds, and dog and shark teeth. Etchings from watercolors by T. Davies, c. 1800.

Below: In a style in stark contrast to the elegance of Choris (p. 2) of the same period, artist Jacques Arago (with Louis de Freycinet on the *Uranie*) illustrates the severity of the "Manner of punishing a criminal in the Sandwich Islands," 1819. Sacrificial victims were often selected from the *kauwā* (outcast class), whose lives were destined specifically for sacrifice.

areas were being cleared for vast fields of taro and sweet potatoes. It is estimated that by 1600 about 80 percent of all land in Hawai'i below fifteen hundred feet had been altered by human inhabitants.

The Hawaiians were building a civilization, not only by use of the land but also by a steady evolution of language, arts, crafts, and culture. Population swelled to an estimated four hundred thousand as their society grew ever more complex. It was not always a peaceful evolution: as small chiefdoms flourished and the chiefs competed for wider control, the warfare could be merciless.

One important chief brought the strife to an end in 1795 when he completed conquest of all the Islands except Kaua'i, which later came into his kingdom via diplomacy. Kamehameha I was the epitome of what it

At Ahu'ena *heiau*, personal temple of Kamehameha I (Kailua, Hawai'i Island), sculptured ritual figures stand tall with imposing authority in 1816. Most of the idols and the *heiau* would come down following abolishment of the *kapu* (prohibition) system just months after Kamehameha's death in 1819. Missionaries from America would not arrive until March 1820. Lithograph after Choris.

"A Man of the Sandwich Islands with His Helmet" (above left) and "A Young Woman of the Sandwich Islands" (above right) depict superb feather work worn only by the *ali'i* (nobility) class. Feather helmets, capes, and cloaks were reserved for men; women of rank wore feather *lei* on the head and/or neck. Only men gathered feathers. Both men and women made *lei*. Engravings from Webber, 1779.

Verdant Hanapēpē Valley on Kaua'i, the first Hawaiian Island to be visited by Cook, 1778. Here, near Waimea village, Cook was first mistaken for the god Lono. As Hawaiians welcomed the Westerners, they became exposed to Western germs. C. Wilkes, 1840.

The young warrior Kamehameha was present when Cook anchored at Kealakekua, 1779, when the major Islands were controlled by several different chiefs. By 1816, when Kamehameha sat for this drawing by Choris, the old warrior was absolute monarch of Hawai'i, Maui, Kaho'olawe, Lāna'i, Moloka'i, O'ahu, and Kaua'i.

Drawing by Wood portrays Kamehameha rehearsing battle skills.

meant to be a Hawaiian warrior-chief—tough, adaptable, clever, and ruthless. Especially important was his adaptability, for he used Western advisors and guns to complete his conquest.

There is a cogent argument that the Spanish knew Hawai'i, for their ships regularly sailed between Acapulco, Mexico, and the Philippines. Spanish galleons generally sailed north or south of Hawai'i, but a map that a British officer captured from the Spanish in 1742 shows the location of two islands, La Mesa (The Table) and Los Mojas (The Monks), in the latitude and relative longitude where the Hawaiian Is-

lands exist—seemingly irrefutable proof that between the years 1556 and 1778 the Spanish were aware of and perhaps had visited Hawai'i. Furthermore, while the feather capes, headdresses, and weapons of Hawai'i were unknown elsewhere in Polynesia, they bear a striking resemblance to those of Spain. The colors most often used in Hawaiian feather capes were red and gold—Spain's royal colors then and now. Finally, in the 1950s (in the Bishop Museum) a hitherto unexamined burial casket from old Hawai'i revealed a piece of iron and a piece of cloth believed to be Spanish sailcloth.

"A Sandwich Island Officer of the King in Grand Costume" by Arago, August 1819. This proud, ranking chief in exquisite traditional regalia also carries the mark of Western influence. The tattoo on his right arm cites the death of Kamehameha, May 8, 1819. Pre-Western contact, Islanders had no written language. His geometric tattoos, however, tell of rank and genealogy.

In any case, the most historically visible stranger to appear on Hawaiian shores was the renowned explorer Captain James Cook. Born in 1746 of obscure parents in an obscure village in Yorkshire, England, he worked as a farmer and as a clerk in a grocery and a haberdasher's shop, then ran away to sea at eighteen. Strong and intelligent, he worked his way up through the fleet and became perhaps the most famous explorer in the world.

During his third and last voyage, Cook brought his ships into the mid-Pacific. He spotted Oʻahu on January 18, 1778, and the next day Kauaʻi and Niʻihau, and he received a friendly reception from the Hawaiians on Kauaʻi. He named the isles the Sandwich Islands, after his patron and friend the Earl of Sandwich. Two weeks later he set sail for America, hoping to find the Northwest Passage. When he failed in that endeavor, he sailed the *Resolution* and *Discovery* back to Hawaiʻi, sighted Maui, and finally anchored in Kealakekua Bay, on the southern shore of the Island of Hawaiʻi. On February 14, 1779, Cook and four marines were killed at Kealakekua in a dispute with some Hawaiians over a stolen cutter. It was a terrible tragedy because Cook, more than some strangers since, liked and respected Hawaiians. He wrote in his journal:

> *Few . . . now lamented our having failed in our endeavor to find a northern passage homeward last summer. To this disappointment we owed our having it in our power to revisit the Sandwich Islands, and to enrich our voyage with a discovery which, though the last, seemed, in every respect, to be the most important that had hitherto been made by Europeans throughout the extent of the Pacific Ocean.*

Cook had opened the door, but his death meant that no ships called in Hawaiʻi for several years, during which time only a handful of Westerners were ashore in the Islands. Marooned British seamen John Young and Isaac Davis became advisors to Kamehameha in the use

Right: Portrait of Captain James Cook, the most highly acclaimed explorer of his time.

Below: "The Death of Captain Cook." From the first encounter between Cook and Hawaiians, iron was a salient subject. Although natives had never known Europeans previously, they did know of iron. They asked for iron, accepted gifts of iron, and pilfered iron. It was this that led to the dispute ending in Cook's death, February 14, 1779. Recording the action, Cook's surgeon David Samwell reported, "... another Indian stabbed (Cook) in the back of the neck with an iron dagger."

Four Russian expeditions visited Hawai'i in the early 19th century. This scene portrays Kamehameha I and his court receiving Captain Otto von Kotzebue and officers from the *Rurick*, Kealakekua Bay, November 1816. Kotzebue assured the king that the Russian government was not interested in establishing Russian colonies in the islands. Lithograph after Choris.

Left: A Roman Catholic priest baptizes High Chief Kālanimoku aboard the French corvette *Uranie* under command of Louis Claude de Freycinet, August 1819, about three months after the death of Kamehameha I. In November 1819, Liholiho (Kamehameha II) would dismantle the Islands' existing religious system. Calvinist missionaries from New England — having left Boston on the brig *Thaddeus*, October 23, 1819 — would arrive in the Islands April 4, 1820, on a mission of conversion.
Painting by Arago.
Below: Carved wooden temple image.

of Western weapons. Other ships came to deal in sandalwood. The wood was cut in Hawai'i, picked up by Western ships, and transported to Canton, where Chinese craftsmen made marvelous boxes and other artifacts from the fragrant wood. This ushered in the era of the traders, who were entrepreneurs of the most daring kind. Two brothers, Captains Jonathan and Nathan Winship, persuaded Kamehameha to give them a monopoly on the sandalwood and to, incidentally, keep the trade for himself. Their contract with the king specified that the king would receive a quarter of all profits. It was one of the early business arrangements between a prominent Hawaiian and men from America, and like some later ones, it did not turn out well for either party. Kamehameha complained that he was being cheated, and the Winship brothers failed to capitalize on the trade to the extent they might have.

In 1793 Captain George Vancouver, who had sailed with Cook, brought Hawai'i's first cattle as a present to Kamehameha, a move that would give rise to

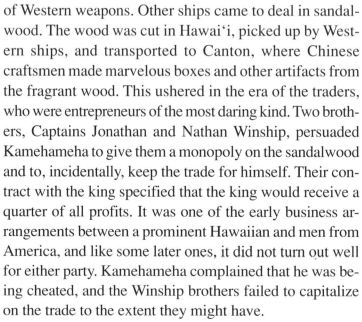

Absence of beasts of burden and the wheel in pre-Western contact Hawai'i, meant that travel anywhere was either by foot or canoe and that transportation of all goods and materials was a manual matter, leading to an athletically arduous lifestyle. Athletic also were several observed sports. Many early accounts cite strong swimming and surfing skills among both women and men.

Left: "Valley of the Pali, near Honolulu," lithograph from T. A. Fisquet, artist on the *Bonité*; with Captain August N. Vaillant, 1836.

Above: Surfing, F. Howard, 1824.

Vancouver, commander of the armed survey ship *Discovery*, assumed an advisory role with Kamehameha I — even arranging what turned out to be a tearful reconciliation between the warrior-king and Ka'ahumanu, his willful and favored wife.

Once Hawaiians realized the purpose and potential of the newly introduced horse, they embraced riding with great gusto. Above: A group of women galloping across the plain below Punchbowl Crater at Honolulu. Wearing voluminous *pā'ū* (skirts) as riding habits continues today as seen in the colorful attire worn for parade riding. Drawing by A. Plume on the *Galathea*, with Captain Steen Bille, 1846.

the ranches of Hawai'i Island, including the vast Parker Ranch. The first horses arrived from California aboard the *Lelia Byrd* as a gift for Kamehameha in 1803, and in 1830 cowboys from Baja California arrived to teach Hawaiians how to manage cattle. Hawai'i developed a thriving cattle industry with colorful and hardworking cowboys.

Other industries followed, geared to Hawai'i's mid-Pacific location. Whaling and the factoring of whaling ships became important to the Islands, especially Maui, where Lahaina flourished as the unofficial whaling capital of the Pacific. Whaling was replaced by sugar in the last quarter of the nineteenth century, which brought workers from China, Japan, the Philippines, and Portugal. The tapestry of the Islands was woven from exotic threads, and the result was a strong and colorful social fabric. Not without its racial incidents and problems, Hawai'i nevertheless developed into a model state for the manner in which different races were able to mix and mingle, to intermarry, and to conduct social and business matters in a spirit of cooperation and harmony. The Islands became, in this respect, the envy of the world.

A Gallery of the Aliʻi

1. King Kamehameha I (1758–1819), in 1819 Louis Choris portrait, was a great warrior and unifier of the Islands. He had vast lands, absolute authority, and an appreciation of Western guns and ships, and utilized *haole* (foreign, white) counsel.

2. Queen Kaʻahumanu (1772–1832), the strong-willed, most-favored of Kamehameha's more than 20 wives, became regent at his death, sharing power with Kamehameha II and, later, with Kamehameha III. By motivating Kamehameha II to overturn the *kapu* system, she changed the course of Hawaiian history.

3. King Kamehameha II (Liholiho, 1797–1824), restless and wanting to see the world, took his wife Kamāmalu to London in 1820. Both died there of measles.

4. Queen Kamāmalu (1800–1824). The king's half sister and favorite wife was a flamboyant figure at home and abroad.

5. High Chief Boki and Chiefess Liliha accompanied Liholiho and Kamāmalu to London, where they proudly wore native dress and sat for this portrait.

6. A pair of Robert Dampier portraits depicting Liholiho's brother and sister, King Kauikeaouli at the age of 12 and the Princess Nahiʻenʻena. As full siblings and the children of Kamehameha I's sacred wife, Keōpūolani, they outranked their father and under the old order would have married each other. Under Christian tenets, this was forbidden, confusing and frustrating both. Nahiʻenʻena died distraught at 21. Later, Kauikeaouli (Kamehameha III) married Kalama.

7. Kauikeaouli (Kamehameha III), 1813–1854, reigned for 30 years, the longest of any Hawaiian monarch. During his reign, Hawaiʻi had three forms of government: the controlled regency of Kaʻahumanu; the autocracy of an out-of-control, unpredictable Kauikeaouli suddenly with real power; and the constitutional monarchy of a more practical-minded king. The *Great Mahele* (system of land division) also marked his reign.

8. Queen Kalama (1817–1870), consort of Kamehameha III, is said to have been well loved by her people.

Colorful Leaders

10.

15.

11.

Despite their noble heritage, the *ali'i* of the late monarchy suffered health problems common to Hawaiians in general of that period. Low birth-rate and early death became the norm. By the time Lili'uokalani came to the throne in 1891, following the death of her brother Kalākaua, the monarchy had but one great hope for an heir — Princess Ka'iulani, daughter of Lili'uokalani's sister Princess Likelike and her Scots husband, businessman Archibald Cleghorn. Fate dealt the dynasty a double blow. Lili'uokalani was deposed in 1893; Ka'iulani came home from years of royal grooming in Great Britain and the Continent to find there would be no kingdom for her to rule. She died, 1899, not yet 24.

10, 11, and 12. Alexander Liholiho (Kamehameha IV), 1834–1863, and his consort, Queen Emma — out of concern for the health of their subjects — founded The Queen's Hospital. Considered very pro-British, they were instrumental in establishing the Anglican Church in Hawai'i. Theirs was an elegant court, a tragic marriage. Their only child, Albert Edward Kauikeaouli, Prince of Hawai'i, died at the age of 4. The king died 15 months later, at 29. As dowager queen, Emma made an unsuccessful bid for the throne following King Lunalilo's death, 1874, but was defeated by Kalākaua.

13. Lot Kamehameha (Kamehameha V), 1830–1872, succeeded his brother Alexander in 1863; adopted a new, less liberal constitution; and worried about the possibility of annexation. He proposed to the widowed Emma (who refused him) and died a bachelor without naming a successor.

14. William Charles Lunalilo (King Lunalilo), 1835–1874, became Hawai'i's first elected king, 1873, when Lot died with no named successor. As king, Lunalilo founded Lunalilo Home for aged Hawaiians. He died unmarried and without naming a successor, one year into his reign.

15. High Chiefess Ruth Keanolani Kanahoahoa Ke'elikolani (Princess Ruth), 1826–1883, refused to convert to Christianity and learned but refused to speak English, leading some to misjudge her considerable intelligence. Her personal life rife with the tragedy of several deaths, she also missed out on gaining the throne but inherited huge amounts of Kamehameha lands, most of which she left to her cousin Pauahi.

16. Charles Reed Bishop, 1822–1915, native New Yorker and astute businessman, married High Chiefess Bernice Pauahi, who would twice refuse the throne and inherit the Kamehameha lands from Princess Ruth. Bishop founded Hawai'i's first bank and, after Pauahi's death, established with his own funds Bernice Pauahi Bishop Museum.

17. High Chiefess Bernice Pauahi Bishop (Princess Pauahi), 1831–1884, as heiress to the Kamehameha estates, founded The Kamehameha Schools/Bishop Estate, becoming Hawai'i's largest benefactor. Her estate totaled approximately 11 percent of Hawai'i's land area. She died without issue.

18. David Kalākaua (King Kalākaua), 1836–1881, in his second bid for the throne, was victorious — he was elected king, 1874, after Lunalilo died without naming a successor. Complex, colorful, and controversial, Kalākaua was forced to accept a new constitution greatly limiting his powers.

19. Queen Kapi'olani, 1834–1899, consort of Kalākaua, stayed at home when the king went on a world tour in 1881, but served as his personal representative in London at Queen Victoria's Jubilee, 1887. Concerned about preservation of the race, she founded a maternity home, now known as Kapi'olani Medical Center for Women and Children.

20. Miriam Likelike Cleghorn (Princess Likelike), mother of Princess Ka'iulani, died mysteriously at age 37. She is said to have made a deathbed prediction that Ka'iulani would leave Hawai'i for a long time, never marry, and never become queen.

21. Archibald Scott Cleghorn, native of Edinburgh, Scotland, and a success in the mercantile business, married Chiefess Likelike and fathered Hawai'i's beloved Princess Ka'iulani. An avid horticulturist, he was renowned for his gardens at 'Āinahau in Waikīkī.

22. Victoria Kawekiu Ka'iulani (Princess Ka'iulani), 1875–1899, heir apparent to the Hawaiian throne until the monarchy was overthrown, 1893.

16.

17.

Fishing in Old Hawai'i

Fishing was paramount in the lives of pre-contact Hawaiians. Terrestrial sources of protein were chronically in short supply; and, surprisingly, "the production of marine food resources near the shores of Hawai'i (has) always been limited and liable to depletion."[2] The latter is true because Hawai'i's isolation limited diversity of its marine life; and Island waters were not nutrient rich because of the Islands' position in relationship to currents and quantity of reef habitat.[3]

Fishing, therefore, was needed on a regular and frequent basis. Men fished singly and in groups; and everything about fishing was interwoven with strict rules and ritual. They developed many ways of fishing — catching by hand, spearing, and noosing; with baskets, traps, hooks, and lines; from shore, underwater, and in canoes. The fisherman's life was strenuous and dangerous. His body of knowledge is said to have been greater than that of the farmer. He had to memorize the undersea terrain both inside and beyond the reef; know currents, weather, the stars, and birds; and, of course, gain in-depth knowledge of each kind of fish. Having to procure canoes and acquire nets and other gear was costly.

Fishermen applied a variety of ingenious techniques and developed great patience in pursuit of fish; they used secrecy and crafty resourcefulness to outsmart fellow fishermen concerning fish habitats and fishing methods.[4] Collective fishing, however — under the direction of a head fisherman — was collaborative. One witness, describing trips in which heavy nets were involved, spoke of 60 canoes, "not fewer than 6000 people, and a catch of 50 or 60 canoe-loads."[5]

Early Hawaiian scholar Samuel Kamakau described a trip to dedicate a new net. Procedures began the day before the trip, with a feast and ritual followed by a *moe kapu*, during which fishermen slept as a group overnight — no one being allowed to sleep at home or lie with his wife. Procedure of the trip was highly structured as was distribution of the catch — who received how much, in what order.[6]

All trips began and ended with prayer and ritual. There were fish shrines, gods for fish, and some *heiau* were dedicated to fishing. Prior to 1819, certain kinds of fish were *kapu* to women. Penalty for *kapu* infraction was death.

1. Fishponds on Kaua'i. Kamakau tells us that fishponds "date from very ancient times"; that they beautify the land; that there were freshwater ponds and shore ponds; and that some ponds were as large as 60 or 70 acres, requiring thousands of men to build.[7] Circa 1800, there were about 300 royal fishponds. Built by commoners, they were managed by keepers appointed by the chiefs. Product of the ponds was primarily for chiefs and *kāhuna*.[8]

2. Modern man fishing with an old-style scoop net made from a pliable wood frame.

3. Torch-fishing with spear and kerosene-fueled torches mirrors the ancient version of the same activity, in which the *lamakū* (torch) was fueled by roasted and shelled *kukui* nuts strung on a coconut frond midrib wrapped in dried *ti* leaves and put in a length of bamboo.[9]

4. Fisherman in a three-man canoe. Indispensable for food gathering, the canoe alone provided pre-contact Hawaiians access to a critical offshore source of protein. An estimated 6,000–12,000 canoes were in use at the time of Cook, 1779.[10]

5. Spearfishing from shore, along the shallows. In ancient days spearfishing was also done while swimming underwater, as well as by torchlight. Typically spears were made of a hardwood pole, six to seven feet long, with a single sharp point.[11]

6. Although ancient Hawaiians used several types of fishing net, throw nets are thought to be a 19th-century import by Japanese fishermen. Ancient nets were made of *olonā*, among the strongest of natural fibers.[12]

The Hawaiian people were a race of expert fishermen.
The art had been handed down from their ancestors ...
passed on by the grandparents to the boys.

— Samuel Manaiakaʻalani Kamakau,[1]
early Hawaiian scholar

Honolulu from offshore in 1848 — a view showing a mix of Hawaiian and Western ways: both thatch and wood architecture; both canoe and tall ship transportation.

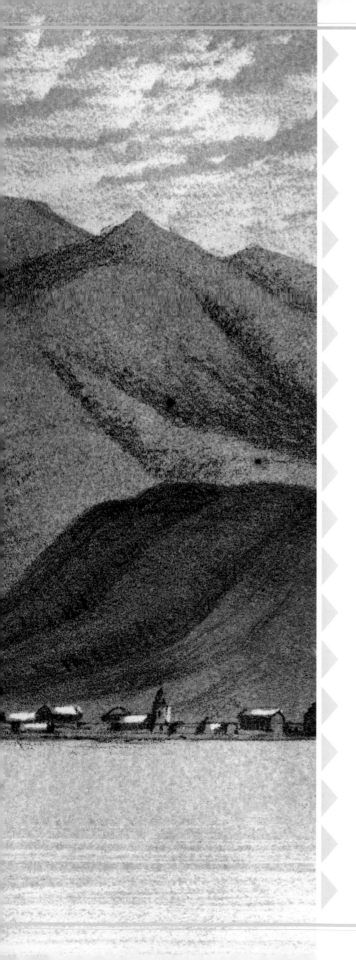

Chapter 2

In 1866 a ship stood off Honolulu Harbor, carrying on board a man with a new name. Samuel L. Clemens had recently taken on the pen name of Mark Twain, and he was on the threshold of making it ever more famous. Now he eyed the place where he planned to spend the next four months writing twenty-five articles for the most famous newspaper in the American West, the Sacramento *Union*. His first impression:

> *On a certain bright morning the Islands hove in sight, lying low on the lonely sea, and everybody climbed to the upper deck to look. After two thousand miles of watery solitude the vision was a welcome one. As we approached, the imposing promontory of Diamond Head rose up out of the ocean its rugged front softened by the hazy distance, and presently the details of the land began to make themselves manifest: first the line of beach; then the plumed cocoanut trees of the tropics; then cabins of the natives; then the white town of Honolulu, said to contain between twelve and fifteen thousand inhabitants spread over a dead level; with streets from twenty to thirty feet wide, solid and level as a floor, most of them straight as a line and few as crooked as a corkscrew.*
>
> *The further I traveled through the town the better I liked it.*

"Vue du port hanarourou," lithograph from Choris, c. 1816. Kamehameha I staunchly upheld Hawai'i's ancient *kapu* system but assertively embraced the ships and guns of the West. The king's fort is central to this image, which includes several of his ships, his coral-stone house, numerous thatch houses, and outrigger canoes.

"Diamond Head from Look-out" provides a close-up of the center area of the map at far right, looking toward the landmark crater.

Right: the fort; highlighted at center, the courthouse; center left: KawaiaHa'o Church, completed 1842. Lithograph from G. H. Burgess, c. 1851.

Hawai'i was beginning to attract people from all over the world, people who came out of curiosity instead of business interest or government necessity. Twain was one of the more famous visitors and one of the early better-known writers. A dozen years later another intrepid writer—this one an intense, no-nonsense Yorkshire woman, Isabella Bird—descended upon Hawai'i after a career of writing about other exotic places, including the Vale of Kashmir, the Upper Yangtze, Tibet, and the deserts of Morocco. She wrote *The Hawaiian Archipelago: Six Months Among the Palm Groves, Coral Reefs and Volcanoes of the Sandwich Islands*, and the world read it with great interest, for Miss Bird wrote comprehensively and well. Like Twain's works, her reports from Hawai'i helped make the world aware of the far Islands in an azure sea. She may have been the first to voice what became a commonplace term for Hawai'i when she wrote:

> *And beyond the reef and beyond the blue, nestling among coconut trees and bananas, umbrella trees and breadfruits, oranges, mangoes, hibiscus, algaroba and passionflowers, almost hidden in the deep,*

dense greenery, was Honolulu. Bright blossom of a summer sea! Fair Paradise of the Pacific!

Among the newcomers to Hawai'i were the missionaries, who came not out of curiosity but to bring their concept of the Supreme Being to the natives. Their impact was deep and lasting in part because of two early efforts—translating the Bible into Hawaiian, and focusing on conversion of the leading chiefs to their beliefs. Like the Polynesians more than a millennium before them,

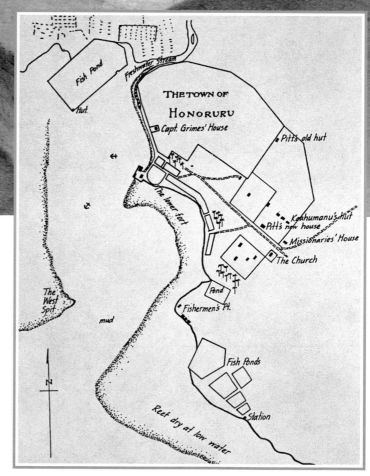

Right: This 1825 map of Honolulu is the work of Lt. C. R. Malden, surveying officer on Britain's HMS *Blonde*, under Captain Lord Bryon, on her voyage specifically to return the bodies of Kamehameha II and Queen Kamāmalu, who had died in London of measles, July 1824. The map records a characteristically Hawaiian element — seven fishponds, thus documenting Islanders' use of aquaculture.

the missionaries were not content with a passive adaptation; they became involved in all aspects of Hawaiian life, and their influence was felt quickly in religion, customs, morals, even dress.

One of the more energetic missionaries did not come from New England, as most had, but from England. The Reverend William Ellis was unlike the Americans in other important ways, primarily in that his writings depicted Hawaiians not as a people in dire need of salvation, but as people of another culture struggling to emerge into modern times.

The Missionaries

It has been said that second only to Cook's accidental arrival, 1778, the most important event in the history of Hawai'i was the arrival of American missionaries, 1820.

It was a time of great religious zeal, but before the missionaries thought of heading from New England out to the Sandwich Islands in search of souls to save, a young Hawaiian of Kealakekua — the very area that had proved fatal for Cook — climbed up the anchor chain of a sailing ship, begging to be taken away to safety from priests who'd held him captive. He was Obookiah (*Opukahaia*), a recent orphan of warfare in which both parents and his infant brother had been killed. The captain took him aboard and, in 1809, to New Haven, Connecticut, where Obookiah lived with the captain's family. There, he was found one day on the steps at the Yale College chapel, "weeping because his people were in ignorance."[1] Students tutored him. A bright, diligent student and ardent Christian, he resolved to return to Hawai'i as a missionary. Several other young Hawaiians showed up, via the shipping path, and expressed interest in study and mission work. Thus it was that the churches there awakened to an evangelical opportunity. In 1816 they founded in Cornwall, Connecticut, a school for the Hawaiians, with the idea of preparing them for the ministry and sending them back to Hawai'i to preach and/or teach. Obookiah's death, in 1819, while still a student, threatened failure for the whole idea, as he was the only one of the group perceived to have the qualities necessary to carry it off. Yet such was the fervor of the New England Calvinists, that they transferred Obookiah's sense of Christian duty to their shoulders, accepting it as their own challenge.

1. Obookiah's dream of Christianizing Hawai'i became viable October 15, 1819, with the establishment by the American Board of Commissioners for Foreign Missions (ABCFM) of the Sandwich Islands Mission. Four days later the new group of volunteer missionaries sailed on the brig *Thaddeus* from Boston, with no expectation of seeing their native land again. Before the ABCFM withdrew its support of the Mission (1845 to 1863), 12 companies had sunk roots in Island soil. Deep and strong in the 21st century, those roots still represent a leadership role in Hawai'i.[2]

2. A sketch of Hiram Bingham, by Bingham, preaching at Waimea during a tour of O'ahu, 1826. The Queen Regent Ka'ahumanu is along to reinforce Bingham's admonitions. Realizing the influence chiefs had on commoners, missionaries began conversion efforts with the *ali'i*. The most influential of them all was Ka'ahumanu, who had led the way in revolt against religious restrictions of the *kapu* system, 1819. Initially, she wasn't anxious to take on the yoke of another set of rules. Patient and persistent, the missionaries were attentive to Ka'ahumanu when she became seriously ill. Gradually she grew attracted to the message of Christ, finally becoming a zealous convert. Just as the missionaries had hoped, she used the full weight of her power and influence, urging others to accept the Christian God.

3. The Reverend Hiram Bingham and his wife, Sybil Moseley Bingham, members of the Pioneer Company of American missionaries, arrived in Honolulu, April 19, 1820. Leader of the Mission, Bingham was pastor and designer of KawaiaHa'o Church; played a major role in creating a written form for the Hawaiian language; translated parts of the Bible into Hawaiian; and became trusted advisor of the king, chiefs, and chiefesses.

24

3.

4.

4. After fourteen years as a medical missionary in Honolulu, Dr. Gerrit Parmele Judd resigned his position as missionary in 1842 to serve the Hawaiian government in a variety of influential roles and to pursue business interests. He became secretary of state for foreign affairs, 1843; minister of the interior, 1845; and commissioner to France, Great Britain, and the United States, 1849. Traveling to these countries, 1849–1850, he took with him two young chiefs who had been educated at the strict missionary-founded Chiefs' Children's School and who would both become king — Prince Alexander Liholiho (Kamehameha IV) and Lot Kamehameha (Kamehameha V).

He was sympathetic to the Hawaiians and intensely interested in the way they lived. As a result, he wrote objectively, and he wrote about things that other missionaries ignored. His journal, published as *Narrative of a Tour of Hawai'i, or Owhyhee*, is a remarkable and valuable piece of work. In it, Ellis wrote about Hawaiian hospitality:

> A transient visitor on arriving among them will generally have an entertainment provided, of which the persons who furnish it seldom partake. The family with which we lodged was, however, induced to join us this evening at supper, though contrary to their ideas of propriety.
>
> Whenever we have remarked to the natives that their conduct in this respect is unsocial, they have usually answered, "Would it be right for us to present food to our friends, and then sit down and eat it ourselves?"
>
> Connected with this, another custom, equally at variance with our views of hospitality, is practiced by the guests, who invariably carry away all that remains of the entertainment, however abundant it may have been. Hence, whenever a pig, &c. has been dressed for us, and our party have finished their meal, our boys always put the remainder into their baskets and carried it away. To this we often objected: but they usually replied, "It is our custom; and if we don't take it, the people will think you are dissatisfied with what they have provided."

The beauty of the Hawaiian women was both a blessing and a curse. Venereal diseases, introduced by Cook's crewmen and subsequently the ships that called

After Russia's ship the *Rurick*, on scientific expedition, visited Hawai'i Island and Kotzebue assured Kamehameha I of Russia's lack of interest in colonizing the Islands, the *Rurick* sailed to Honolulu. There, Choris, in his 1816 sketch "*Port d'hanarourou*," portrayed an active village still under *kapu* control but adopting Western imports — notably cows and horses.

Seven years later, in describing the same locale, William Ellis (insert left) wrote: *Immediately south of the valley of Anuanu (Nu'uanu) is situated the town and harbour of Honoruru; the harbour is the best, and indeed the only secure one at all seasons, in the Sandwich Islands, and is more frequented by foreign vessels than any other; seldom having within it less than three or four, and sometimes upward of thirty, lying at anchor at the same time ... On the eastern side of the basin is a strong fort, one hundred yards square, mounting sixty guns. It was begun by the Russians, who were expelled, but finished by the natives, from an apprehension that these foreigners ... were about to take possession of the island.*[3]

Hula, the Dance of Life

Hula at the time of early Western contact was a visual rendering and/or enhancement of Hawai'i's oral literature. Without knowledge of Hawai'i's language, poetic conventions, and cultural and religious traditions, it was impossible to understand and appreciate the *hula*.

Because the language was without written form, memory plus oral presentation assumed the duties written languages typically perform. It might be said that Hawai'i's oral literature functioned for Hawaiians very much as, for instance, Shakespeare or the Bible serve English speakers: recitation of genealogies; stories of all kinds; history; songs of joy and awe; prayer; lamentation; and praise of gods, men, and women. As Adrienne Kaeppler, a writer of music and dance, explained:

(Hawai'i's) music was a complex integrated system of poetry, rhythm, melody, and movement that served many functions, from prayer to entertainment. The most important and basic element of this complex was the text. Rendered melodically and rhythmically, the poetry could be interpreted on more than one level ... dance rendered this poetry into visual form by alluding to selected words of the text ... The dancer was essentially a storyteller ... conveying the text depended primarily on movement of the hands and arms.[4]

Hula was an integral part of Hawaiian life. *Hula* existed as performance art or entertainment; as spontaneous activity for pleasure; as magic in ritual form; and in celebration or honor of people or events. There were casual performers, roving professionals, dedicated students at *hālau hula* (schools) who lived under rigorous religious *kapu*, and dancers who belonged to a chief's court. There were appropriate *hula* for any kind of occasion, from conception and birth to death. Hawaiians dealt with these issues openly, without self-consciousness. *Hula*, Hawai'i's dance of life, barely survived the Western onslaught. The miracle is: it did.

1. "*Iles Sandwich: Femme d'Isle Maui Dansant.*" A Maui dancer performs a *hula kuhi lima* (seated dance without instruments, emphasizing arm movements). Elaborately tattooed from the waist up, she wears a voluminously draped *pā'ū*. Arago, 1819.

2. "*Danse des Femmes,*" Choris with Kotzebue on the *Rurick*, 1816. Fashionably coifed in the favored short hair of the period and wearing short, intricately draped and tied *pā'ū kapa*, a large group of female dancers entertain Western guests and natives.

3. "*Danse des Hommes*," Choris, 1816. Sporting both long and short hairstyles, carrying feather-decorated shields, and wearing boar-tusk bracelets and dog-teeth anklets (in reverse position of the single dancer's, below), tattooed male dancers wear short garments similar to the women's but without the bustle effect. They are accompanied by musicians playing large gourd drums and small probably coconut shell drums. A high-ranking woman sits in the front row with a *kāhili,* a feather standard.

4. A presumed ceremonial dance is performed by a single tattooed male with a feather gourd rattle, wearing a *malo* (loincloth), a collar-like necklace, and leg cuffs decorated with rows of dog teeth attached to *olonā* cording. The cuffs probably acted as rattles. Lithograph after Webber sketch, 1778.

"*Scene de Danse aux Iles Sandwich*," by Barthéleme Lauvergne, depicts a festive entertainment flaunting the *hula* for the *Bonité* crew, when the French man-of-war put in at Honolulu, 1836. By then such occasions were rare and, by contemporary reports, lacking the spirit of earlier times. Not only had the dance costume become Westernized, the number of performers had dwindled, and the dance itself had lost much of its former vitality. Adolph Barrot,[5] of the *Bonité*, said, "Only the singing and the singers appeared to have preserved all the originality of ancient times ... (the dancing was) mean and monotonous ... far from realizing the idea we had formed of it." The motivating force behind the changes was commented on by Charles Wilkes,[6] writing (c. 1840) that dance in Hawai'i had been "interdicted" by missionaries "in order to root out the licentiousness that pervaded the land. They therefore discourage any nocturnal assemblies ... The watchfulness of the government, police, and missionaries is constantly required to enforce the due observance of the laws."

Above: "*Jeune femme des Iles Sandwich dansant*," lithograph after Arago. This bare-breasted, seated dancer seems to emerge from voluminous puffs of her *pā'ū* settled low around her hips. Around her neck is a *lei palaoa*, icon of chiefly status, and she is missing a tooth. Usually this indicates a self-inflicted loss to mourn the death of an *ali'i* — in this case quite possibly the passing of Kamehameha I, whose death, May 8, 1819, preceded Arago's visit by only three months.

from all over the world, began the great decline of the Hawaiian population. Cook tried to keep his sailors separated from the Hawaiian women, but it was impossible, as the ship captains who followed Cook also discovered. Between 1820 and 1840—busy years for Pacific whaling—the incidence of diseases among the Hawaiians peaked. The Hawaiians had no natural immunity to diseases that killed them—influenza, mumps, smallpox, whooping cough, scarlet fever, and others. Certainly there was no immunity to the terrible venereal diseases that raced like wildfire through the populace.

The Reverend Hiram Bingham was in charge of the first company of missionaries that the American Board of Commissioners for Foreign Missions sent out from Boston. He was successful in converting many of the higher-ranking chiefs and chiefesses, and he won their approval to declare it taboo for Hawaiian women to visit the ships. One ship's captain who fumed at this ruling was the skipper of the *Dolphin*, Lieutenant "Mad Jack" Percival, whose vessel was the first American warship to visit Hawai'i. That was in 1826, and Percival's crew and a few other hangers-on rebelled at the taboo and rioted at a missionary worship service. Bingham described the scene:

> As we were assembling for worship,
> in and around the house of Kalanimoku,
> in the afternoon, several seamen, part of
> whom belonged to the Dolphin, rushed
> into the spacious hall or saloon in the sec-
> ond story where were Kaahumanu,
> Kalanimoku, Namahana, and Boki, and a
> considerable number of others, and with
> menacing tones and gestures made their
> demands and threats. "Where are the

Right: On a hill above the port of Lahaina, Maui, the Reverend Lorrin Andrews founded Lahainaluna Seminary, 1831, for Hawaiians. In early years of Hawai'i's whaling boom, Lahaina Christians — some of them Hawaiian — managed to keep tighter control of liquor licenses than their counterparts in Honolulu. For a while this resulted in fewer whalers calling at Lahaina than at Honolulu.

women? Take off this tabu, and let us have women on board our vessels, or we will pull down your houses. There are 150 of us—the tabu must come off: there is no other way." Thus commenced a riot which occupied the time and place of the expected divine service. These were followed by successive squads. One and another dashed in the windows of Kalanimoku's fine hall, breaking some seventy panes along the veranda. Some, I think, did not intend violence; and one of them said to me, "I wish you to take notice who they are that are doing this; we are not all engaged in it."

Above: This aquatint after Hulsart details the action of the famous Roach fleet among a shoal of sperm whale off Hawai'i Island, 1833.

The rioting spread to Bingham's house and became more intense before some Hawaiians came to the rescue, attacking the sailors. Finally, Lieutenant Percival arrived on the scene and calm was restored, but the riot had its intended effect. Bingham continued:

In the evening of the same day the commander waited on the chiefs and reiterated his objections to the tabu, and, while he admitted that the sailors had gone too far, expressed his unwillingness to leave the country till his vessel should enjoy the privileges that had been enjoyed by the vessels of other nations. Governor Boki and Manuia, the commander of the fort, whose effective agency were then essential to the enforcement of the tabu, yielded to its violation in the harbor of Honolulu.

The whalingmen's impact on the Hawaiians was deep and often confusing. The Hawaiians noted the worth of the goods flowing in and out of the ports of Lahaina and Honolulu and observed the excesses of the whalingmen ashore, and all the while their own values crumbled. They lost much of their land and watched as their population dwindled from at least 400,000 down to about 135,000 in 1823. Having lost the *kapu* system that had framed their lives, the Hawaiians were bewildered and hard-pressed to make sense of their lives and time.

The missionaries, for all their good intentions and sincere zeal, also brought some prejudices and conflicting ideals, so that for a span of time the Hawaiians were torn between the whalingmen and the missionaries, unable to anchor their beliefs and their spirituality.

It was a critical time that continued for decades. The missionaries outlasted the whaling era and ultimately had a deeper impact on Hawai'i than the whalers. But even after the whaling era ended in the 1870s, the malaise in Hawai'i did not. In 1887, King Kalākaua grieved over

A cosmopolitan collection of ships characterized Honolulu's bustling harbor in 1892. The Kingdom was in a chaotic political state. Queen Lili'uokalani was considering a national lottery to boost needed revenue, while Hawai'i's native population was in serious decline due largely to introduced germs to which Hawaiians had no immunity.

In an act not likely to have happened pre-1819, two Hawaiian women make *poi*, the nutritious staple derived from the root of the taro plant, first brought to the Islands in the canoes of the original settlers. Before the *kapu* system was overturned, *poi* making was a man's job; and women were not allowed to eat with men.

the condition of his people. In an introduction to Kalākaua's book, *The Legends and Myths of Hawai'i*, R. M. Daggett noted (with the king's approval):

> *In the midst of evidences of prosperity and advancement it is but too apparent that the natives are steadily decreasing in numbers and gradually losing their hold upon the fair land of their fathers. Within a century they have dwindled from four hundred thousand healthy and happy children of nature, without care and without want, to a little more than a tenth of that number of land-less, hopeless victims to the greed and vices of civilization. They are slowly sinking under the restraints and burdens of their surroundings, and will in time succumb to social and political conditions foreign to their natures and poisonous to their blood. Year by year their footprints will grow more dim along the sands of their reef-sheltered shores, and fainter and fainter will come their simple songs from the shadows of the palms, until finally their voices will be heard no more forever.*

"Dance We Will"

"Dance We Will — No Tabu!" As early as 1821 — just one year after the arrival in Hawai'i of missionaries with their vehement protests against *hula* — Oahu's Governor Boki uttered this defiant outcry against the Reverend Hiram Bingham's admonition against including *hula* in the mourning ceremonies to be held for two *ali'i* on a Sunday.[7]

The incident would come to characterize a conflict of over 50 years between missionary forces doing everything in their power to eradicate *hula* and Hawaiians, who kept dancing whenever and however they could. When powerful Queen Ka'ahumanu converted to Christianity and subsequently forbid *hula*, it survived largely underground, with the exception of periodic court performances supported by several monarchs. Even then, it was *hula* performed in missionary-approved costumes designed to conceal a great deal of what dancers had been schooled to reveal. The tide turned with the accession of David Kalākaua, who inaugurated an assertive cultural revival that continued throughout his reign, 1874–1891. Following him, Queen Lili'oukalani was of like mind in cultural matters. Both were musically gifted, missionary-educated, politically controversial Royalists who in their musical responses became bellwethers. While cherishing the Hawaiian language and traditional music and dance, they remained open to new instruments (*'ukulele*, guitar, piano) and new kinds of music (melody and harmony of hymns, brass band).

Actively participating in the blending of these cultural elements, they served as strong forces in the amalgamation of the traditional and the in-troduced, which resulted in a form now recognized as "Hawaiian music."[8] The 20th century saw widespread, albeit often superficial, fascination with Hawaiian music and dance. In mid-century, Elvis rocked on stage with his own style of pelvic movement, and for a decade *hula* lost the limelight. In the 1960s, indigenous culture became cool; sex was no longer sinful; and *hula* arose Phoenix-like from the hearts of folk who had harbored it all along. In the 21st century, *hula* thrives in a contemporary form and in an evolved traditional form amongst thousands of adherents in Hawai'i and in a growing body of initiates on the U.S. Mainland, and in Japan and Mexico.

1. Out of hiding, into public — *hula* at Kalākaua's 50th birthday Jubilee, 1886, where a *hula* dancer was accompanied by *'ukulele*. The audience loved and the "merrie monarch" sanctioned the new music.[9]

2. Studio *hula*, 1870s. Even before Kalākaua's Jubilee "revival," *hula* was a favorite subject of photographers, striving to capture Hawai'i's exotic appeal with fully clad dancers in front of backdrops.

3. *Hula* dancer in lush *lei maile*, amply covered from neck to knees, including long, puffed sleeves. She is free of leggings and shoes, possibly signifying a later date than 1870s.

4. Men and women *hula* dancers posed together, 1896, wearing raffia skirts introduced from the Gilbert Islands. Blouses have become more brief.

5. By the 1920s and 1930s the idea of *hula* was so seductive that young women with no connection to *hula* liked to dress up in *hula* costume. By then skirts were usually "grass" or cellophane.

5.

6.

4.

8.

9.

7.

7. The Merrie Monarch Festival epitomizes the *hula* renaissance begun in the 1960s. Held annually in Hilo, the three-day competition for *hālau hula* is a statewide occasion that sells out months in advance.

8. Hālau Hula Ka Pā Hula O Kamehameha, Merrie Monarch Festival, 2002. Male *hula* continues to gain favor, especially in the vigorous *kahiko* style of dance.

9. Hālau Hula Olana, Merrie Monarch, 2002. Other major annual *hula* events include the Kamehameha Schools Hula Competition and the noncompetitive Prince Lot Hula Festival held each summer at Moanalua, O'ahu, on a site where *hula* was performed in ancient times.

6. During World War II *hula* was a huge hit with servicemen. Ti-leaf skirts gained popularity in the 1940s and remain so in the 21st century.

It was one of the introduced diseases that proved devastating to Hawaiians — exactly from where or when it came is not recorded. Natives called it *ma'i Pākē* (Chinese disease). Whites identified it as leprosy. In 20th-century Hawai'i it came to be called Hansen's disease, reflecting the name of the man who identified the *bacillus leprae*. By any name, it signified dread, disfigurement, and painful death, until the introduction of sulfone drugs in the 1940s. Hawai'i's Leprosy Act, 1865, provided for segregation of victims, and the village of Kalawao on Moloka'i's Kalaupapa Peninsula was made a settlement site where patients were forcibly sent. For the following century — until the Board of Health ended the segregation policy in 1969 — more than 7,000 men, women, and children lived out involuntarily confined lives there. Before the priest Damien arrived, 1873, settlement residents were essentially left to survive on their own amid disgraceful, lawless conditions. The more fortunate were accompanied by a *kō kua* (helper), usually a spouse or relative. Many, including children, had to fend for themselves. Notable among volunteers who dedicated their own lives to aid the outcasts were: Father Damien de Veuster; Brother Joseph Dutton; and Mother Marianne Cope.

1. Heroic figure — now a candidate for sainthood — Father Damien Joseph de Veuster (1840–1889), a Belgian priest who voluntarily committed his life to the exiled patients of Kalawao/Kalaupapa.

2. By 1960, the settlement at Kalawao was an organized and tidy community. Today the peninsula is the site of Kalaupapa National Historic Park, a home and haven for those patients who wish to be there. They are free to come and go at will — by air.

3. Damien with female patients thought to be members of a choir he organized, possibly the first Kalaupapa photograph, mid-1870s.

4. The boys of Baldwin Home, c. 1895, lovingly cared for by Brother Dutton for 44 years.

5. The Baldwin Home Band by Damien's church, Kalawao. Music was — and remains — an important part of life at the settlement, which moved from Kalawao to Kalaupapa village over a period of several years beginning about 1887.

6. Baseball — one of many games and organizations that Father Damien, Brother Dutton, and Mother Marianne organized to help patients achieve a sense of normalcy and feelings of accomplishment and joy.

2.

Hawaiian Ranching
AND THE PANIOLO

Ranching in Hawai'i is one of those things "new" to the Islands — in this case an introduced industry — that has become Hawaiianized, making the import very much at home. With ranching, it's not so much in the cattle or the horses that the uniqueness stands out but rather, in the cowboys — the *paniolo* — and their culture.

What are the distinguishing features of *paniolo* culture?

To begin, there's the multi-heritage mix of various Polynesian, Western, and Asian backgrounds, which accounts for physical differences and the lilt of voices that carry signatures of different language families. Originally ranching's primary language was Hawaiian; and ranch vocabulary remains well larded with Hawaiian words.

Paniolo, building from a base of Hawaiian traditions and values, honed a lifestyle that incorporates bits and pieces of other represented cultures. For example, traditionally bareheaded Hawaiians learned that the Spanish-Mexican *vaqueros'* big-brimmed *sombreros* served a highly useful purpose during long days on the range. Taking advantage of already well-developed Hawaiian weaving skills, Hawaiians' love of *lei*, and availability of several choice materials, *paniolo* "metamorphosed" the floppy *sombrero* into intricately designed, handwoven *lau hala* (pandanus leaf) hats of a variety of sizes and shapes, with hatbands in a choice of lovely *lei* — flower, feather, or shell. Reportedly, old-time *paniolo* took special delight in wearing *lei*, especially *lei maile*, while at work.[10]

Then there is the *paniolo* "talk story" tradition; the *himeni paniolo* (cowboy anthem) they sing; and the music they play on *'ukulele* (developed in Hawai'i from the Portuguese *branguiha*, often made of *koa* or other local wood) and guitars. Most often, they were tuned *ki hō'alu* (slack key — tuning in an old, formerly "secret," way), a distinctly post-contact,

seductively sweet Hawaiian technique. Make no mistake, Hawai'i's *paniolo* are every bit as rugged, capable, and stalwart as the hard-riding Spanish-Mexican *vaqueros* that Kamehameha III imported in 1832 to teach Hawaiians the rigorous skills of riding, horse breaking, steer roping, branding, castrating, herding, and moving cattle from shore to ship. Although the imported cowboys were Spanish, Mexican, and Indian, to Hawaiians they were all Spanish — *espagniolos* — thus, in Hawaiian, *paniolo*. A trio of *paniolo* made steer roping history in 1908 when Ikua Purdy won the World's Steer Roping Championship in Cheyenne, Wyoming, while Archie Kaaua took third place and Jack Low sixth place.

1. David Kuloloia, *paniolo*, at 'Ulupalakua on Maui, 1930s. His wide-brimmed, handmade *lau hala* hat and *palaka* (checkered) cloth shirt distinguish him as a Hawaiian cowboy.

2. Roundup in big sky country — big sky over Waimea, Hawai'i, at Parker Ranch, 1950s, where 225,000 acres; 50,000 head of cattle; and 400 working horses establish it as the largest family-owned ranch in the U.S.

The ranch was founded by John Palmer Parker, a pioneering, ambitious, and enterprising former New Englander who — becoming truly enthralled with Hawai'i and its people — made an invaluable business connection with Kamehameha I in 1815 and somewhat later married a granddaughter of the chief. The arrangements worked well for all concerned. Parker's marriage to Kipikane (formalized first by a *kahuna* in traditional Hawaiian ritual and much later in a Christian ceremony) was rock

solid. He ran his business operation based on New England industry and Hawaiian cultural mores. Parker learned the language and even became adept at chanting. His interest in and commitment to Hawaiian culture helped form the basis for a ranch *'ohana* (family), notable for loyalty, mutual respect, and admiration. By all reports, Parker Ranch, under John Palmer Parker and Kipikane, established a template

for a new lifestyle in Hawai'i, a cultural "marriage" that we recognize still.

3. Kailua-Kona, 1939. Before long piers were built, getting cattle to market in Honolulu from neighbor islands entailed a dangerous process of "swimming" cattle from shore to ship. This technique was introduced by the Spanish-Mexican *vaqueros* who came in 1832 to teach Hawaiians cattle ranching's multiple tasks. The first step, after herding the animals to the beach, is to tow each steer through the surf to a waiting longboat ...

4. ... At the longboat, five or six steers are cross-tied to each side of the boat and thereby hauled out through sometimes shark-infested water to a waiting ship, where each steer is lifted aboard for the trip to Honolulu. Offshore Kailua-Kona, Hawai'i.

Contract laborers recently arrived from Japan, 1889, to augment sugar plantation labor needs. Men greatly outnumbered women, as most men intended to return to Japan with saved earnings following completion of their contracts. Some did; many more sent for families or "picture brides," who came by mail-order arrangement to work in the fields and to marry men they knew only by photograph. Over 60,000 Japanese were living in Hawai'i in 1900. The men on horseback are Caucasian *luna* (field bosses), and were often accused of being overly harsh.

Chapter 3

Cook's arrival threw cultures into conflict. In less than fifty years there were other white strangers on the Islands, never to depart. They came as sea captains, traders, whalingmen, missionaries, entrepreneurs, and often as drifters. They brought new ideas, new ways of thinking, and new and sometimes bewildering behaviors.

From Scotland came the most tenacious and hardworking of the new arrivals. They came to work on and manage the sugar plantations that sprang up after the demise of whaling, most arriving between 1880 and 1930. They and their descendants would make a lasting impact on the business and social life of the Islands.

"Hawaiian Neptune," Keaukaha, Hawai'i. An 1850 law mandated work for contract laborers and Hawaiians. Refusal could result in "prison at hard labor ... (As) late as 1874 *Kanaka Maoli* (full-blooded Hawaiians) were being prosecuted for *ha'alele hana*, abandoning work."[1] Fishing and *hula* were more compatible with their culture. This early 20th-century fisherman, standing by an intercoastal canoe, models traditional attire: *malo* and *'ahu ua* (rain cape made of ti leaves).

Two elegant Chinese beauties with an American flag as a backdrop, perhaps symbolizing dual pride, 1914.

Other Europeans turned up—six hundred Scandinavians came beginning in 1881, but most did not stay, preferring other climates and other lifestyles. Some fourteen hundred Germans arrived, as did some Russians, Greeks, and Italians. By 1853 there were some sixteen hundred whites in Hawai'i, but a quarter century later there were almost thirty thousand—20 percent of the population. By the new millennium whites made up close to 25 percent of the Islands' total population.

From the Atlantic Islands of Portugal came the Portuguese. In 1878 their migrations began in earnest when the German bark *Priscilla* docked after 116 days at sea, bringing 120 Portuguese contract workers for the sugar plantations. From 1878 to 1913 there were twenty-nine voyages, bringing almost twenty-six thousand people. By 1980 there were at least fifty-five thousand people in Hawai'i of Portuguese ancestry. They brought the instrument that would become the *'ukulele*; dances like the *chamarita*; and foods such as *malasadas*, *pao doce*, and *bulo de mel*. Without them, it was said, the Islands would be *uma mesa sem vinho*, a table without wine.

Steerage aboard the SS *China*, 1901.

As fresh as it gets — live as well as plucked poultry and produce at Sing Mow market, 112 N. Hotel Street, Honolulu, where proprietor Chun Mow Bew had living space upstairs. In time, sons Soy Sun, Soy Hooh, and Soy Cheong joined him in business.

Center: One small boy amid a large multiracial group of women plantation workers, Kilauea, Kaua'i, 1888. Gathered for the photograph in the sugarcane field where they toil, these women earned far less than their male counterparts for the same number of hours in the field.

Often management kept workers segregated by race in different camps to lessen the likelihood of laborers bonding in opposition to management.

Above: Said to be from the Big Island of Hawai'i, this Chinese family represents proud accomplishment as a photographer snaps them before a painted backdrop.

Among the three hundred or so foreigners in Hawai'i at the start of the nineteenth century, there was a handful of Chinese. But in 1852 waves of Chinese immigrants, primarily from Guangdong and Fujian, were brought in to work the sugar plantations. They boarded ships to Hawai'i willingly, for their own land, torn by the Tai Ping Rebellion, was under the leadership of a mystic who proclaimed himself to be the younger brother of Christ. The entrepreneurial Chinese tended to work out their contracts then move into the city to open their own businesses. With the Treaty of Reciprocity in 1876, which spurred sugar production by offering tariff advantages to Hawai'i sugar growers, even more Chinese arrived, and they began to intermarry. In the new century more than 60 percent of them married into another race. Over the course of two hundred years, more than forty thousand Chinese came to Hawai'i, to make a mark as strong as the brush stroke of calligraphy. They were the first of the Asian immigrants to the Islands, and their accomplishments are legion. Today they make up 5 percent of Hawai'i's population.

Above: A Portuguese get-together. Typically, early Portuguese families in Hawai'i were large. They came as plantation contract laborers. Church, family, and community defined their character.

Formal *kimono* and the young woman in traditional Japanese headdress suggest a Japanese wedding photograph. Hairstyles of the two standing young women suggest a 1920s time frame.

The second group of Asian immigrants came from a kingdom that was famous for its isolation long before it became famous for other things. From the shadow of Mount Fuji came the first Japanese immigrant workers in 1868, called the "first-year persons" because they arrived during the first year of the Meiji Restoration. The Meiji Restoration marked the end of the power of the Tokugawa Shoguns and the opening of Japan, which had been closed to foreigners since 1633. The initial group of Japanese workers found work-related problems too difficult to overcome and returned to Japan. However, in 1885 the ship *City of Tokyo* brought 943 Japanese to Hawai'i as *Kanyaku Imin*, contract workers for the plantations. King Kalākaua himself went down to meet the ship.

In the years to come the Japanese saw America, fearful of too much foreign labor, close its door to Asian citizenship and Asian immigration. Japanese males were not much inclined to intermarry anyway, and the years 1908–1920 became the era of the "picture brides," young Japanese women brought on contract to Hawai'i to marry

A young Korean family. The father moves ahead in a thoroughly modern American suit; the mother maintains tradition in decorous Korean dress. Posing before a romantically conceived backdrop, they stand on a practical Hawaiian *lau hala* floor mat.

The sleeves and hats tell the story: the lovely ladies celebrate the culture of the Philippines.

Chinese immigrant Ah In, a Pālama, Honolulu, rice farmer, imported Hawai'i's first water buffalo from South China in the 1880s. This buffalo works a paddy with a farmer in McCully, an area adjacent to Waikiki.

Japanese men. The Japanese population increased so that by 1920 more than 40 percent of Hawai'i's population was Japanese. In a century, Hawai'i's Japanese population climbed to more than a quarter of a million. Individual Japanese rose to positions of power, becoming prominent in politics, labor unions, and government. In time the first non-Caucasian governor of Hawai'i would be an American of Japanese ancestry. By the early 1990s in Hawai'i, people of Japanese ancestry represented nearly 25 percent of the population.

In 1882 America was the first Western country to make a treaty with an ancient land of tough and energetic people, a place called The Land of the Morning Freshness. Korea was suffering political unrest, and the Korean emperor saw greater opportunities for his people in Hawai'i. On January 13, 1903, about one hundred Koreans arrived in Hawai'i to seek their destinies. They looked beyond the plantations for opportunities; within three years there were more than forty-five hundred Koreans in Hawai'i, noted for their high degree of literacy and their willingness to intermarry. In the second half of the twentieth century they became one of the larger immigrant groups, all upwardly mobile, highly adaptable, and retaining their inherent energy and strong will.

The Filipinos came to Hawai'i with musical languages and a propensity for hard work. Their immigration began in 1906, and like others they came because of unrest in their own country and opportunities in Hawai'i. The Spanish-American War had just ended, and the U.S. was left in charge of the Philippines. There seemed no reason why Filipino laborers could not be recruited and many reasons why they should. Despite poor pay and working conditions for them in the Islands, by 1930 there were more than sixty thousand Filipinos in Hawai'i. Some went on to the U.S. Mainland, some returned to the Philippines, but many stayed. After World War II there

The exotic pineapple, long a symbol of hospitality, was introduced in Hawai'i by Don Marin, 1813. The Islands' climate and rich soil made the Hawai'i/pineapple "marriage" a perfect match; but learning how to successfully grow great fruit, and to harvest, preserve, and market it, took the rest of the 19th century. The industry began to take off about the beginning of the next century. By 1920, O'ahu, Moloka'i, Maui, and Kaua'i had pineapple plantations. "Canned pineapple was the territory's second industry, accounting for almost all of the world's output." By 1929, James Dole's Hawaiian Pineapple Company had turned Lāna'i into one big plantation, and his Iwilei cannery in Honolulu was the world's largest.[2]

With a background of the steep, etched Koʻolau range, acres of undulating pineapple fields define central Oʻahu's landscape.

Before mechanization supplanted manual labor (c. 1930s), field hands picked the prickly fruit and carried it in shoulder slings to the nearest field road, where it would be picked up.[3]

was another surge to Hawaiʻi, as more than seven thousand Filipinos made the journey to the Islands that earlier generations had made. The Filipinos are credited with the success of the pineapple and sugar plantations, but they did not confine themselves to the production of agriculture. As years passed the Filipinos began to have a more profound impact on the political and social events taking place in Hawaiʻi.

Other groups came to Hawaiʻi in lesser numbers, including African Americans, Native Americans, Fijians, Laotians, Pakistanis, Tahitians, and Indonesians. The hardy people of Southeast Asia came, repeating the route of the Polynesians across the Pacific to Hawaiʻi. They are not overwhelming in numbers, but they add exotic touches to Hawaiʻi's social and cultural life. Like those who arrived before them, they show little reluctance to intermarry. In a recent year, 46.5 percent of all marriages in Hawaiʻi were interracial, and 60 percent of the children born in Hawaiʻi that year were of mixed blood. Overall, about 33 percent of Hawaiʻi's people are of mixed race, a figure that is expected to continue to rise. In a book published a few years ago, *He Mele O Hawaiʻi*, the author put it this way:

> *There is something else that must be said about them, something that is mirrored in their productivity, their social consciousness. It is the fact that in*

In cadence, against clatter, a line of neatly uniformed packers carefully inspect and grade pineapple slices, then place them in the appropriate cans.

For half a century or more, during the summer peak of the canning season, Island students by the hundreds found ready employment at the cannery, a job many in the 21st century recall as noisy, grueling, uncomfortable work. Gloves, they report, failed to protect their hands from the sticky, irritating juice.

In 1903, Hawaiian Pineapple Company's first pack, at Wahiawā cannery, central Oʻahu, netted 1,893 cases. Their Iwilei cannery's first pack, 1907, netted 2,250,000 cans.

the sun-washed Islands they put aside their prejudices to create an atmosphere of tolerance, a sense of focus on the important things of life. They accomplish this in a variety of ways involving academics and religion and simple propinquity, but mostly they have done it by marrying each other.

The people came together in a way that was miraculous, and not a collective miracle but one that took place individually, in each untrammeled heart. They reached across barriers of color and custom, leaped across the barricades of intolerance to embrace each other in a kind of acceptance that did not seem to be occurring anywhere else. No attempt was made to disguise their differences; rather each of them found something in those dissimilarities to admire and enjoy. It was as if each decided that the other was exotic rather than eccentric, and in

Already in the Islands when Captain Cook arrived, *kō* (sugarcane) would eventually play a major role in the history of Hawai'i. Not only did sugar become, and remain, the number one industry for many years, the industry's labor requirements became the impetus for importation of a labor pool from numerous nations — east and west — establishing a basis for Hawai'i's characterizing multiracial composition. Further, the sugar industry was a factor in political complexities leading to the overthrow of the monarchy and subsequent annexation to the United States. Waipahu sugar plantation and mill, O'ahu.

Work in the cane fields required care and protective clothing from razor-sharp leaves.

Large numbers of field hands inspired entrepreneurial instincts among the labor force. This vegetable farmer takes her offering of fresh produce directly to cane workers at the Waimānalo plantation, Oʻahu. She uses the ancient carrying device — two baskets hanging from opposite ends of a long pole balanced across her shoulder.

surrendering their xenophobia, each found a freedom to associate, to encompass, to love.

This was the miracle; that it happened one-on-one, not by ukase and not en masse, but in the tentative turning of one soul toward another, individuals free to abandon false pride while keeping the best of their heritage. The people of these fortunate islands were blessed with a clarity of vision that permitted them to appreciate individualism. The islands themselves linked the people in a commonality of beauty and gave them the rich loam of tolerance in which to plant the seeds of their futures. And while the islands gave them freedom their own histories gave them perseverance, and their own genes gave them strength, and their own spirits gave them an acceptance of the time and place and circumstances, so that in the end there were no strangers in paradise, but only others superficially unlike themselves, but very much alike in all the ways that mattered.

And what of the Hawaiians, the sons and daughters of the first immigrants? Notwithstanding King Kalākaua's fears, the voices of the Hawaiians did not fall silent, nor have they disappeared. In a survey taken in the early l990s, approximately 207,000 people in Hawai‘i reported they had some Hawaiian blood, and the same survey reported 9,417 pure Hawaiians. All of the immigrant groups that came after the Polynesians have played out their lives and destinies against the backdrop of a land infused with Hawaiian culture and customs. The very rocks, hills, and streams of Hawai‘i seem to speak with the voices of the land's first people.

It is true that the Hawaiians fell victim to the outsiders' diseases, first the physical ones, then the psychological ones. There was an era of low self-esteem, when one's worth was measured in the classrooms. Academically, the Hawaiians were bright, but they lacked confidence and tended to drop out in difficult situations, a kind of withdrawal that other Hawaiians understood but other races often misinterpreted. The Hawaiians suffered from a high mortality rate brought on by diets that worsened as they abandoned the splendid health practices of Old Hawai‘i. Happily, in recent years, the outlook for the Hawaiians has brightened.

The considerable intermarriages of the Hawaiians with other races may have diffused the bloodlines, but they also disseminated throughout the modern community some of the Hawaiian attitudes, practices, and ideals that might otherwise have been diminished or even disappeared. The intermarriages increased the awareness of what it meant to be Hawaiian among diverse people. Without the intermarriages there might not have been the strong cultural renaissance that Hawaiians have experienced in the decades leading up to the millennium, a renaissance that cut across all ethnic and age groups and survived long enough to ensure it would continue. Indeed, the call of some Hawaiians for a form of sovereignty is an outgrowth of a newfound pride in being Hawaiian, and it heralds a strong voice from the Hawaiian community as it moves into the future.

Old-style native cooking — no deep-frying and no women in the "kitchen." Men cooked (pig, fish, chicken, dog, bananas, sweet potatoes, yams, taro, and breadfruit), steaming food long and slowly in an *imu* (underground oven) with hot rocks.

Portrait of Mele Kaupoko, a symbol of cultural struggle, wearing a somber all-covering, missionary-imposed garment while the *lei palaoa* around her neck and the feather *kāhili* in her hand proclaim chiefly status.

Indigenous architecture, imported livestock. The preferred thatching material for "grass houses" was *pili* grass. Thatch over the doorway remained untrimmed until the house was ready for occupancy. Then a ceremonial cutting of the *piko* (navel cord) of the house was performed and the thatch cut.[4]

Above: Charles Kauha (per J. A. Gilman, Jr.) exhibits two native proclivities that would have been sternly discouraged by missionaries — "wasting" time at the beach surfing and wearing almost no clothes.

Right: "Native Taro Vender," in Western garb, carries a load of the indigenous, labor-intensive crop, taro — both root and tops nutritious.

Ali'i Lifestyles

In the Hawai'i of pre-Western contact, distinction between classes was extreme, with the *ali'i* class, the aristocracy, holding — and exercising — the power of life and death over lower classes. Change began with the arrival of tall ships from Western nations, became monumental with the abolishment of the *kapu* system, 1819, and continued with the coming of American missionaries. All things Western were superimposed on a nation that was, in large part, open to change. Class distinctions changed — but not completely. Until the end of the 19th century, Hawai'i remained a monarchy. The *ali'i* remained nobility. Conditioned for centuries by genealogically determined power, privilege, and prestige, this state of being was the natural order of things for them. It was theirs by birth, the masses serving and paying homage to them. Throughout the profound changes affecting all phases of Hawaiian life, chiefs and chiefesses had a life and lifestyle distinct unto them and their retainers. Encroaching ideas of democracy notwithstanding, a palpable difference prevailed between *ali'i* and *maka'āinana*, the people of the land.

1. As in Hawaiian music, with its different layers of meaning, this impressive social event has more to say than its surface glamour. Seen at center, with a *kāhili* being waved over her head, is the bright, beautiful Princess Ka'iulani — or ex-princess — who had been groomed to rule, presiding as hostess of a large and lavish formal dinner at 'Āinahau, her home in Waikīkī. The time was October 1898, two months after the raising of the American flag over 'Iolani Palace. The occasion feted members of the Annexation Commission appointed by U.S. President William McKinley to assess Hawai'i, America's new territory. Was Ka'iulani resigned to the loss of her country's independence and her own loss of status as future queen? Evidence suggests the grand affair was part of loyalists' futile efforts to restore the monarchy. Ka'iulani would never be queen. Less than six months later she would be mourned as Hawai'i's lost

hope, dead at 23.

2. Horseback riding in the country — Princess Elizabeth Kahanu Ka'auwai and husband Prince Jonah Kūhio Kalaniana'ole, late 19th or early 20th century.

3. This royal outing at John A. Cummins's Waimānalo country house includes three princesses of the Kalākaua dynasty (left to right, seated in chairs): Ka'iulani (age thirteen), Lili'uokalani (heir apparent), and Po'omaikelani (sister of Queen Kapi'olani, Kalākaua's consort).

4. On February 3, 1889, a *lū'au* at the Waikīkī cottage of Henry E. Poor honored visiting author Robert Louis Stevenson and group and was further distinguished by having royal guests. At the head of the table (left to right, seated): Stevenson; heir apparent Princess Lili'uokalani; King Kalākaua; and Mrs. Thomas Stevenson, the writer's mother. The menu is said to have included Island favorites — raw and cooked fish, crab, *limu* (seaweed), chicken, pig, *poi*, roasted *kukui* nuts, and baked dog.

5. Princess Ka'iulani as a child, posing in front of a painted Diamond Head.

6. Nalani Jones and Princess Elizabeth Kalaniana'ole relaxing at the beach, Koko Head in the background.

7. Near the *lānai* (porch) at 'Āinahau (left to right): Prince David Kawananakoa (Ka'iulani's cousin and possible suitor); Eva Parker (of the Big Island Parker Ranch family of royal and *haole* genealogy); Rose Cleghorn (half sister to Ka'iulani); and Princess Ka'iulani, back home following eight years of "finishing" in England and on the Continent, 1898.

8. King David Kalākaua and Queen Kapi'olani with retinue in front of the new 'Iolani Palace, completed in 1882. Though most of his subjects were still living in thatched houses, the Renaissance revivalist palace well characterizes the influence of European architecture on Hawai'i's mid-19th century royalty. Behind the king and queen stand acting chamberlain Colonel Sam Nowlein and Antoinette Swan, daughter of Don Francisco de Paula Marin.

The Reign of Kalākaua

As an elected sovereign of a constitutional monarchy who governed as though he believed in the divine right of kings, Kalākaua was easily maligned. Extravagant, self-indulgent, and notably unpredictable and capricious — especially about changing ministerial appointments, dismissing Caucasian ministers and replacing them with Hawaiians — his reign was rife with controversy, scandal, and turmoil. Eventually, the sugar interests would prevail, forcing him to sign a new constitution (known as the "Bayonet Constitution") that transferred power to the legislature, severely limiting the king's power.

Beyond politics and poker games, however, the man Kalākaua was a scholar, a poet, a composer of music that lives today, and — above all — a stalwart supporter of Hawaiʻi's traditional culture and arts, particularly the *hula*. It is this legacy that distinguishes him and by which he is appreciated and honored in the 21st century.

1. King David Kalākaua, 1836–1891, married Kapiʻolani (granddaughter of Kauaʻi King Kaumualiʻi), 1863. He was elected king by the Hawaiʻi legislature, taking oath of office February 13, 1874.

2. The Reciprocity Commission: (seated) Governor John Dominis, King David Kalākaua, Governor Kapena; (standing) H. A. Pierce, Luther Severance. After long, complicated negotiations, Kalākaua accepted Reciprocity Treaty details giving Hawaiʻi favorable trade terms on sugar and other items in exchange for U.S. "coaling station rights" at Pearl Harbor. It became operative September 9, 1876, and was celebrated in Hawaiʻi with "an all night torchlight procession and fireworks."[5]

3. Throughout his 17-year reign, Kalākaua steadfastly encouraged the open practice of traditional *hula*, to the great disapproval of missionaries. In this scene, a large crowd gathers at the Palace for a performance of *hula ʻōlapa*, a dance accompanied by chanting and drumming on a gourd — part of Kalākaua's coronation festivities, February 1883 (sometimes credited as a Kalākaua Jubilee event, November 1886).

4. With dreams of an empire — a federation of Pacific Islands with Hawaiʻi at the helm — Kalākaua bought and refitted a trading steamer, commissioning it as the *Kaimiloa*, 1887, to carry an embassy to Apia, Samoa. The effort proved to be inept diplomacy, failing miserably. Here Kalākaua, on the bridge, surveys his navy, composed in part of boys from the Honolulu Reformatory School.

5. The HMS *Kaimiloa*, flagship of Kalākaua's ill-fated navy, at anchor.

6. Lover of life, liquor, and lavish *lūʻau*, Kalākaua stands proudly in regal trappings of European monarchial style.

7. Fire station draped in mourning at Kalākaua's death. He died of a stroke in San Francisco while on a rest and recuperation trip, January 20, 1891, at 54, without issue.

2.

3.

4.

5.

6.

7.

HALOHIA KA MAKUA

Flower Lei

1. De rigueur for political campaigns are plenty of *lei*, and it was no different in 1915. This campaign junket included (left to right): Representative Carter Glass; Speaker Holstein, House of Representatives (Hawai'i); Hawai'i Delegate to Congress Prince Jonah Kūhio Kalaniana'ole; Representative Phil Campbell, Kansas; and Honolulu Mayor John C. Lane.

2. Graduation time places a huge demand for flowers on growers; prices inevitably rise. Hawai'i School for Girls at La Pietra, 1975.

3. Always crowd pleasers — fabulous floral *pā'ū* riders and their *lei*-laden mounts give the June Kamehameha Day parades a uniquely Hawaiian character, 1980.

4. In Hawai'i, May Day is indeed Lei Day — a festive day in schools and throughout communities. The city and county of Honolulu sponsors a *lei*-making contest, which inspires newly created *lei* designs each year. Of course, no one is too young to celebrate Lei Day, 1981.

5. The heroic bronze-gilded statue of Kamehameha the Great, presiding in front of Ali'iōlani Hale on King Street, Honolulu, becomes spectacular when draped from fingertip to fingertip with dozens of 20-foot *lei* for each Kamehameha Day, 1980.

6. *Lei* sellers, c. 1901. As late as the 1950s *lei* sellers in the Mō'ili'ili area of Honolulu habitually added a few extra — and free — flowers to any purchase.

7. The association of *lei* with festivity is so ingrained that when the occasion calls for glitter, it likely takes *lei* form, December 1981.

8. A Christmas *lei*, 1916 — The Queen's Hospital nurses stand for a group photo after a carol serenade for patients.

9. No outrigger canoe race would be complete without *lei* for the paddlers. Outrigger Canoe Club's women's crew, September 1981.

The Executive Building,
formerly 'Iolani Palace,
festively lit and arrayed in
bunting to honor the
United States fleet, 1925.
The first lighting of the
Palace was in 1886.
Queen Lili'uokalani (right)
was deposed in 1893.
Hawai'i became a U.S.
territory August 12, 1898.

Chapter 4

As Queen Liliʻuokalani looked out over Honolulu, she saw a city of contradictions. It was still a sailors' rough port, but it had a few paved streets and sidewalks. The *lūʻau* torches still burned, but there was gas lighting in some of the buildings. By 1887, ʻIolani Palace itself had gas lighting.

Lei-bedecked Company Two (last of the volunteer fire departments) and a decorated fire engine as a float, about to join a Jubilee event, November 16, 1886, celebrating King Kalākaua's 50th birthday. Festivities lasted a week and included a parade, regattas, and *lūʻau*.

Prince Jonah Kūhiō Kalanianaʻole and Princess Elizabeth Kahanu Kaʻauwai Kalanianaʻole in an early automobile, around the turn of the century. He served as elected delegate to Congress from 1903 until his death, 1922.

The days of barter were gone, for the kingdom now had its own currency, ending the confusion of previous years when myriad coins from many nations were exchanged in Honolulu shops. There was a police force, a fire department, a library, public parks, an ice plant, and a handful of hotels for the ever-increasing visitors. The queen may have pondered the future of her kingdom; her own life as a queen was drawing to a close. The Hawaiian monarch who was closest to her people lost her throne. She was made to swear allegiance to a new government and to sign her abdication as queen of Hawaiʻi. Honolulu became capital of a territory of the United States on August 12, 1898.

After annexation, the Organic Act of 1900 made citizens of all Hawaiians. Hawaiians became the majority voting bloc—Asians laborers could not vote—but Caucasians dominated the business and political scenes. Many of the Caucasians were conservative Republicans, and some were descendants of the missionary families.

The city itself continued to evolve. On several streets, mule-drawn trams made for smooth and easy transportation. The Cathedral of Our Lady of Peace provided a venue for Catholics, who could now worship freely, having once been persecuted for their faith. (The early Protestant missionaries convinced the chiefs that Catholicism was subversive, so lay Catholics were tortured and priests banished until a French warship arrived to support the Catholics, intimidating the Hawaiian leaders into granting Catholics rights to worship and expand).

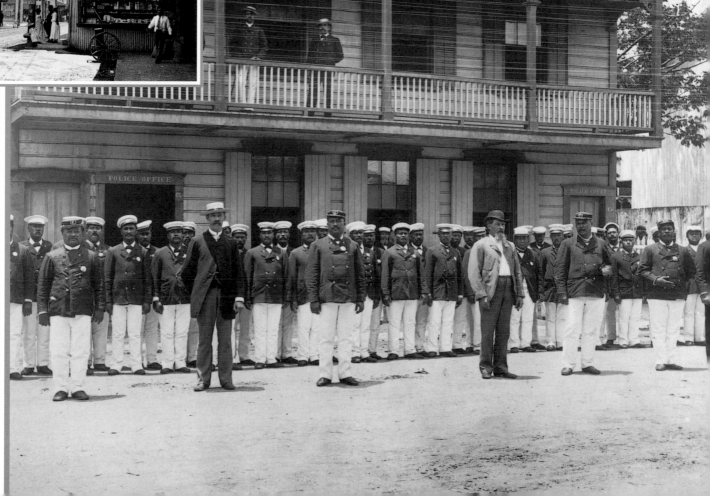

Inspection of Honolulu's police officers in front of the King Street building that housed the police department and district court, 1885 or 1886.

Inset top: Passengers all dressed up for a horse-drawn trolley ride on the "Road to Waikiki," 1901.

Inset bottom: The wheel was nonexistent in ancient Hawai'i. In this downtown Honolulu photo, 1901, there are three kinds of wheeled conveyances: buggy, bicycle, and cart.

A Kingdom Lost

The "Bayonet Constitution" of 1887, diluting the power of the throne, resulted in resentment among Hawaiians and effectively set in motion a political situation that was precarious by the time Lili'uokalani came to the throne at the death of Kalākaua, 1891. When she was deposed only two years later, Lili'uokalani's position was one of perseverance. She continued to look for ways to restore the monarchy. She held President Grover Cleveland in high esteem; his report to Congress, December 18, 1893, gave her hope. Herewith are excerpts from that speech:

... but for the lawless occupation of Honolulu under false pretexts by the United States forces, ... the Queen and her Government would never have yielded to the provisional government ...
Believing, therefore, that the United States could not ... annex the islands without justly incurring the imputation of acquiring them by unjustifiable methods, I shall not again submit the treaty of annexation to the Senate for its consideration ...
By an act of war, committed with the participation of a diplomatic representative of the United States and without authority of Congress, the Government of a feeble but friendly and confiding people has been overthrown. A substantial wrong has thus been done which a due regard for our national character as well as the rights of the injured people requires we should endeavor to repair. The provisional government has not assumed a republican or other constitutional form, but has remained a mere executive council or oligarchy, set up without the assent of the people. It has not sought to find a permanent basis of popular support and has given no evidence of an intention to do so. Indeed, the representatives of that government assert that the people of Hawai'i are unfit for popular government and frankly avow that they can be best ruled by arbitrary or despotic power ...

1. The Royalist Surrender.

2. Following Lili'uokalani's failed attempt to promulgate a new constitution overturning the constitution of 1887, a group of annexationists formed the Committee of Safety, which deposed the queen on January 17, 1893, and formed a provisional government. This was followed by sending an annexation committee to Washington, asking for territorial status within the United States. The committee included: L. A. Thurston, W. C. Wilder, W. R. Castle, J. Marsden, and C. L. Carter.

3. After annexationists created the Republic of Hawai'i from the provisional government, July 4, 1894, Royalists made a failed attempt to restore the monarchy the following January. The former queen was arrested at her Washington Place home, January 16, 1895, and brought to the Executive Building — her former Palace — where she was escorted in, flanked by Captain Robert Waipa Parker, Deputy Marshall Arthur Brown, and Colonel J. H. Fisher. There she was confined in quarters on the second floor, awaiting trial.

4. "Paul Neumann making his address on behalf of the ex-Queen at her trial in the Palace." Drawing from a photo that appeared in the *San Francisco Examiner*, February 16, 1895.

5. The ultimate goal of the annexationists culminated August 12, 1898, with the transfer of sovereignty changing the Republic of Hawai'i to the Territory of Hawai'i. In ceremonies at 'Iolani Palace, "Hawai'i Pono'i," anthem of an independent nation, was played; the Hawaiian flag was lowered, the U.S. flag took its place; and the "Star Spangled Banner" was played. Hawaiians became Americans. To Hawaiians it was "the ultimate dispossession."[1]

6. The United States Navy Bluejackets and marines from the USS *Philadelphia* come ashore to attend annexation ceremonies.

7. President Sanford Ballard Dole (left) transfers sovereignty of the Republic of Hawai'i to United States Minister Harold M. Sewall (right) as Hawai'i becomes a territory of the United States.

1.

THE ROYALIST SURRENDER.

The Cabinet were summoned to surrender the Palace, Police Station and Barracks. They endeavored to gain time, but the Provisional Government insisted upon an immediate unconditional surrender. The Police Station was accordingly given up at once, the Queen retiring from the Palace and the barracks being taken into possession the next day. The Cabinet note the following protest:

I, LILIUOKALANI, by the Grace of God and under the Constitution of the Hawaiian Kingdom, Queen, do hereby solemnly protest against any all acts done against myself and the Constitutional Government of the Hawaiian Kingdom by certain persons claiming to have established a Provisional Government for and for this Kingdom.

That I yield to the superior force of the United States of America whose Minister Plenipotentiary, His Excellency John L. Stevens, has caused United States troops to be landed at Honolulu and declared that he would support the said Provisional Government.

Now to avoid any collision of armed forces, and perhaps the loss of life, I do under this protest and impelled by said force yield my authority until such time as the Government of the United States shall upon the facts being presented to it undo the action of its representative and reinstate me in the authority which I claim as the Constitutional Sovereign of the Hawaiian Islands.

Done at Honolulu this 17th day of January, A. D. 1893.

(Signed)	LILIUOKALANI, R.
(Signed)	SAMUEL PARKER,
	Minister of Foreign Affairs.
(Signed)	WM. H. CORNWELL,
	Minister of Finance.

4.

NEUMANN MAKING HIS ADDRESS ON BEHALF OF THE EX-QUEEN AT HER TRIAL IN THE

2.

L. A. THURSTON. W. C. WILDER. W. R. CASTLE. J. MARSDEN. C. L. CARTER.

3.

6.

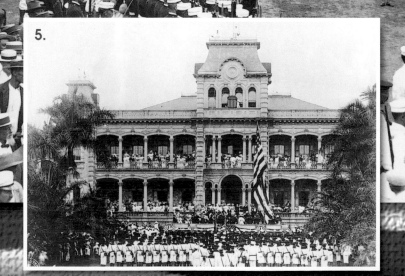

5.

7.

8. Of the time she was brought to trial, Lili'uokalani later wrote, "My equanimity was never disturbed; and their own report relates that I throughout preserved 'that haughty carriage' which marked me as an 'unusual woman.'" [2]

Queen Liliʻuokalani

"Suddenly, the midwife moved with the *kahuna*... The child was born quickly and the *kahuna* blessed it immediately and almost surreptitiously, for *kāhuna* were not yet welcome where missionaries might appear at any moment."[3]

Already the defining cadence of her life was in play. Opposing elements would be a constant refrain as she struggled to balance Hawaiian *aliʻi* traditions with rigid, guilt-focused Christian Congregational mores.

Born Liliʻu Kamakaʻeha, September 2, 1838, to Keohokalole (of high chiefly descent) and Kapaakea (from a line of chiefly warriors), within hours she was taken as *hānai* (foster) daughter to Konia (high chiefess and granddaughter of Kamehameha the Great) and Paki. There she spent her first three years embraced by traditions of chiefly rank before being placed — against her will — in the boarding school for chiefs' children under the direction of missionaries who gave her the "Christian" name Lydia Paki.

Earlier, as was the custom, Konia had composed a name song for the infant *aliʻi*, by which she was "given" many blessings of nature — fruits, flowers, rain, the verdant beauties of Nuʻuanu Valley. A splendid heritage for a royal princess this was, and indicative of Hawaiian values and concepts of "ownership" of such wealth — "it could never be hers entirely, for it was shared by all, from 'forest goddesses' to the 'being' of a rainbow lei for *pili* grass."[4]

Ultimately, Konia's nonmaterial, spiritual legacy would come full circle in Liliʻu's own legacy to the world — the music of her heart.

Her music would also be her lifelong joy, her solace, the mitigating resolution to the dissonance that was her destiny. In her words, "To compose was as natural to me as to breathe; ... this gift of nature ... remains a source of the greatest consolation..."[5]

1. Lydia Paki, about 15. Intelligent, musically gifted, contemplative, and determined, she experienced bouts of unwarranted guilt.

2. As a young woman High Chiefess Lydia Paki/Liliʻu Kamakaʻeha enjoyed swimming, surfing, and moonlight horseback rides; *lūʻau*, picnics, and parties, where extemporaneously composed *mele* (songs) and chants were part of the fun.

3. With her marriage (September 16, 1862) to John Owen Dominis, High Chiefess Liliʻu Kamakaʻeha became merely Mrs. John Dominis. She signed letters and music "Liliʻu Kamakaʻeha." When her brother David became king, she became "Princess Kamakaʻeha Dominis." It was not until the death of her brother Leleiohoku that Kalākaua declared her heir apparent and gave her the name by which the world knows her — "Liliʻuokalani." She called it "no name at all."

4. The *ʻukulele* thought to have belonged to Liliʻuokalani and cover sheet of one of hundreds of her compositions.

5. John Owen Dominis, Jr. (1832–1891), consort of Liliʻuokalani and governor of Oʻahu.

6. Berger and band, c. 1887. Heinrich Berger, bandmaster, who came to Hawaiʻi on loan from Kaiser Wilhelm I at the bidding of Kamehameha V, made a name for himself as he turned a ragtag group of undisciplined boys into a highly polished Royal

7.

8.

10.

11.

12.

6.

9.

Hawaiian Band. He, further, established a rewarding relationship with Lili'uokalani. In Berger, she found someone with whom to share the music of her life.

7. Queen Lili'uokalani (center, seated), members of the royal family, her court, and retainers on a summer outing at the queen's country place at Waipi'o — 1892, during the most crucial period of her political life.

8. Princess Lili'uokalani in conversation with author Robert Louis Stevenson following a *lū'au* honoring the Stevensons. Waikiki, February 3, 1889.

9. In 1916, still *mō'ī wahine* (queen) to her followers, Lili'u emerges from her former palace, reportedly the only time she entered 'Iolani Palace after being imprisoned there following the overthrow.

10. Former Queen Lili'uokalani at end-of-year exercises, 1914, St. Andrew's Priory, a private school for girls. For years she tried unsuccessfully to found a school for girls. She did start Queen Lili'uokalani's Children's Center on behalf of neglected children. She died without issue but with three *hānai* children.

11. Indomitable Lili'uokalani, 1914, 21 years after being deposed, appears in public with Sanford B. Dole (left) who had been instrumental in her overthrow. At right, then-Governor Lucius E. Pinkham. The occasion, to boost patriotism, had been arranged by the queen's longtime friend Henry Berger (standing).

12. A poignant moment during ceremonies, April 1982, at the unveiling of Lili'uokalani's sculpture, when a dancer presents her *ho'okupu* (tribute) with tears in her eyes.

The Anglican St. Andrew's Cathedral was being built, a century-long task. The deposed Liliʻuokalani still lived in Washington Place, and nearby was Aliʻiōlani Hale, site of the judiciary.

Between the Palace and the harbor, the streets of Honolulu were being wired for telephones, telegraph, and electricity. By April 1901 the Stangenwald Building rose six stories over Merchant Street. There were even a few flush toilets. There were photo studios and a skating rink. The first automobiles, both electric, arrived on October 8, 1899, and a year later an auto ran two bicyclists off the street at the intersection of King and Kalākaua Streets, likely the first auto accident in Hawaiʻi.

The area that had been a yam field belonging to Kamehameha I grew into a business spread encompassing King, Alakea, Beretania, and Nuʻuanu Streets.

Where need was great — the Seamen's Bethel Church, established 1833 in the midst of Honolulu's roiling waterfront area (now King and Bethel Streets), was specifically for seamen and was the first church for non-natives. Lost to the fire of April 18, 1886, its congregation melded into what became Central Union Church, still perceived as the Protestant church of early *haole* residents.

KawaiaHaʻo Church as a stone edifice was preceded by several thatched versions before being completed, 1842, under the direction of missionary Hiram Bingham, on the site of his first — and *the* first — Honolulu sermon in English. The scene of royal baptisms, marriages, and funerals, KawaiaHaʻo became known as Honolulu's church of royalty.[6]

Above: Anglophiles Alexander Liholiho (Kamehameha IV) and wife, the Chiefess Emma Rooke, were instrumental in bringing the Anglican Church to Hawai'i. Established in 1862, O'ahu's first Episcopal church building was a modest wooden structure built on crown land within walking distance of 'Iolani Palace. It was superceded by St. Andrew's Cathedral, which took almost a century to complete.[8]

The completion of Our Lady of Peace Catholic Cathedral, 1843, in downtown Honolulu on land given by Kauikeaouli (Kamehameha III) represented far more than a physical landmark. Catholic priests had been expelled in 1831, and native Catholics were harshly persecuted until 1839, when the French frigate *Artémise* landed at Honolulu and Captain C. P. T. Laplace demanded complete religious freedom for Catholics, backing up his demands with the threat of bombarding Honolulu.[7]

A 1932 aerial view of the University of Hawai'i in Mānoa Valley.

The street names reflected the life of the times: Beretania was named for the British influence. Queen was named for Queen Kalama, wife of Kamehameha III. Miller Street honored the first British consul general, while Church, Chapel, and KawaiaHa'o Streets were all named for KawaiaHa'o Church. A sailors' church, Bethel, lent its name to another street, while Alakea (white street) was named for its white coral paving.

Leeward of downtown was Chinatown, where almost seven thousand people—mostly, but not all, Chinese—were crammed into fifty acres. In that teeming area in the waning days of 1899 a case of bubonic plague was reported, and the Board of Health decided on a "sanitary burning" that meant Chinatown's citizens were sent to live in quarantined areas on the outskirts of town. On January 20, 1900, a "sanitary fire" that had been set near Beretania Street and Nu'uanu Avenue was wind-whipped across rooftops and out of the reach of firemen. Citizens fled in panic. A column of dense black smoke rose over the city, and smaller fires sprang up. Before it was brought under control, the fire destroyed thirty-eight acres of Chinatown, a devastating blow to a great number of residents. Thousands of Chinese and other residents were forced to live in quarantine camps, and claims against

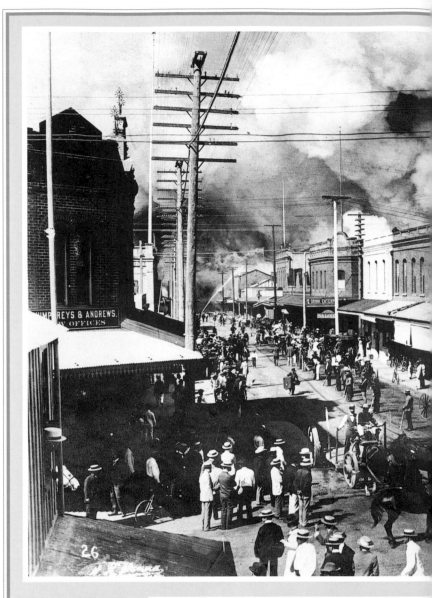

Right: A purging of the plague, December 1899. Following confiscation of their personal effects, and forced antiseptic baths in open-air, makeshift facilities, these men received new clothes and, here, line up to be sent on foot to quarantine camp at the Kaka'ako Rifle Range. Women and children went in wagons.

Above: Downtown Honolulu during the Chinatown fire, January 20, 1900. Right: Honolulu firemen in action, January 20, 1900. The Kaumakapili Church and Sing Kee Grocery store are in the background.

Above: Honolulu had two major Chinatown fires. The first was accidentally ignited Sunday afternoon, April 23, 1886, when a group of gamblers received word police were approaching. Trying to destroy the evidence of their activity, they stuffed a stove with lottery tickets. In short order one mistake led to another, which led to the frame building's bursting into flame, igniting the whole tinderbox neighborhood of wood buildings. The fire destroyed almost 60 acres; nearly 7,000 people, mostly Chinese, were left homeless. Structural loss was 523 buildings including the Bethel Church and the Honolulu police station.[9]

the government were not settled for months. The ousted residents of the area claimed the fire had been allowed to spread to give the Caucasians more room to expand businesses downtown.

The Great Chinatown Fire was one of the seminal events of the early twentieth century. It was followed shortly by a profound event—as World War I ensued, Hawai‘i had to look hard at its mid-Pacific location and begin to think in geopolitical terms.

The war had a depressing effect in Hawai‘i. The Islands became fevered with anti-German sentiment, to the point that schools demanded a loyalty oath, and persons with German-sounding names were inspired to change them or hide them. German language courses were dropped from school curricula. There were some unwarranted persecutions, and for many Islanders the end of the war could not come soon enough. Adding to the tensions, the military flooded Hawai‘i. Fort Shafter became an important army complex, and Schofield Barracks grew to be the largest army outpost in the world. More and more ships were in the sea lanes in and around Pearl Har-

Above left: In seven languages, this World War I poster hawks U.S. government war savings stamps.

Left: If Honolulu firemen looked Hawai‘i-casual wearing *lei* on their way to the king's birthday bash (p. 69) in 1886, these men of the Makiki fire station earn plaudits by knitting scarves for American soldiers on the European battlefields during World War I efforts, 1918.

Right: Big crowds and the Stars and Stripes galore in downtown Honolulu. American patriotism is on parade during World War I, with a Pearl Harbor group in the foreground.

bor. Civilian-military tensions smoldered, occasionally flaring into criminal acts on one side or the other.

The tensions simmered down to an uneasy truce. Civilians recognized the economic impact of federal dollars, while the military grew to appreciate Hawai'i as an outpost. Incvitably, the old trade of prostitution flourished along with dozens of new military-connected businesses, and the trade continued in Hawai'i long after the end of World War I. Meanwhile, some in both the military and civilian camps came to recognize that the two communities could live in harmony if they only understood each other a little better, and efforts were made—particularly by the Chamber of Commerce of Hawai'i—to mend fences. Military expenditures were growing to become a vital part of the economy, and would remain so, and the young servicemen and the local people were learning to tolerate each other. Nobody, at the time, had any idea that in the near future there would be a repetition of the military "invasion" of Hawai'i on an even grander scale, and that the reason for it would begin with a shattering surprise attack on military bases in the Islands.

2.

1.

3.

1. A pastoral Waikīkī, c. 1880, with Diamond Head in the background, and in the foreground that isle insignia — a line of coconut palms. One coconut grove in Waikīkī is said to have had 10,000 trees.

2. Waikīkī Beach stretched out in panorama during halcyon days, as it blossomed into a popular resort for well-to-do travelers after the opening of the five-story Moana Hotel, 1901. This busy day at the beach was probably in between 1910 and 1920. The Royal Hawaiian would open in 1927, and the Moana pier would be removed in 1930.

3. Beach scene, c. 1946 — postwar exuberance prevails: World War II is over; the Japanese are defeated; the "swimsuit police" are defeated; and the navy is out to do reconnaissance duty.

4. Artist's rendition of Kamehameha the Great's 1795 landing at Waikīkī with his fleet of warriors, who subsequently prevailed in the battle for Oʻahu. A reenactment of the historic event was staged for the grand opening of the Royal Hawaiian Hotel, 1927. The same event had also been commemorated in a 1910 pageant.

5. Two men with fishing canoes at Waikīkī Beach, c. 1890.

6. Decorous beach attire for women, c. 1905. By 1913, some women swimmers were ready to break ranks by wearing more practical garb — boys' swimming suits — a practice the mayor riled against, proposing a law forbidding it.

Nature's abundant blessings positioned Waikiki to be a chosen place. Early chiefs of O'ahu chose Waikiki as their seat of power because it offered the best of land and sea: a wide reef-protected bay and beach for their canoes; accessible fishing grounds; freshwater streams feeding rich wetlands advantageous to agriculture and aquaculture; and, for pleasure, cooling trade winds and fine waters for surfing and swimming.

When, in 1795, Kamehameha the Great conquered O'ahu he, too, chose Waikiki, establishing his court at a site where the Royal Hawaiian Hotel would later rise as center of the modern resort area. In time, the warrior-king acquired Western vessels, requiring a deeper harbor than Waikiki provided. He then moved his court westward to the port of Honolulu, keeping a compound in Waikiki for purposes of pleasure. The cool breezes afforded a respite from the dry, dusty plains of Honolulu; and Kamehameha is said to have enjoyed surfing at Waikiki. Reports say his wife Ka'ahumanu and retainers enjoyed themselves there.

Was this the first use of Waikiki as a resort? It would seem it may have marked the beginning of a concept about Waikiki that remains essentially unchallenged two centuries later — that it's a great place to go for rest and renewal. Many 19th-century chiefs and chiefesses after Kamehameha had principal houses in central Honolulu, augmented by beach houses at Waikiki, where relaxed informality prevailed over the more formal protocol of Honolulu. Among the *ali'i* who acquired homes in Waikiki for retreat and casual living were: Kamehameha IV; Kamehameha V; King Lunalilo (who willed his to Queen Emma); Princess Bernice Pauahi Bishop; King Kalākaua with Queen Kapi'olani and Queen Lili'uokalani. Archibald Cleghorn, the Scots businessman who married Princess Likelike and became the father of Ka'iulani, last heir to the throne, had a large Waikiki estate where he built the fabled 'Āinahau. Sometimes in the evenings, the ill-fated Princess Ka'iulani and friends would go for a cool "bath" in their nightgowns in the waters of Waikiki.[10]

7. Reflecting the spirit of the times between World War I and World War II, a group of Mainlanders and Islanders display a joyful, playful innocence as they embrace superficial Hollywood/Tin Pan Alley/vaudeville versions of Hawaiiana. Authentic it wasn't; but the world loved it, and Hawai'i became the fantasy of millions.

7.

Since those days, a century has brought vast change, especially in terms of density, accessibility, and complexity. Wars, politics, technology, economic conditions, climates elsewhere, and marketing techniques each play a role in the ongoing scenario. It is not without its detractors. Withal, Waikiki as playground steadfastly continues to capture the imagination of residents and visitors. The urban resort that is the Waikiki of the 21st century may be characterized by its built environment. Its power — *mana*, if you will — still derives from its natural environment, which, ultimately, has its way with Hawai'i's people, endowing them with an undeniable something special often called *aloha*.

1. Swimming and surfing legend Duke Paoa Kahanamoku, 1890–1968, with his koa and redwood board, c. 1930s. "The Duke's" position in the history of world-class athletes was recognized in 2002, with a U.S. postage stamp bearing his image. Duke spent most of his life living in Waikiki, in the role of consummate waterman and ambassador of *aloha*. He brought international recognition to the Islands with Olympic medals in 1912, 1920, 1924, and 1928.

2. Aerial of Waikiki, between 1927 and 1930. The newly completed Royal Hawaiian Hotel presides in isolated splendor on the site where Kamehameha I established his court after conquering O'ahu.

3. Symbolic of things to come, the Famous Sikorsky 42 — first of the large flying boats to cross the Pacific in connection with Pan American's exploratory flights — passes Diamond Head as it

travels along Waikiki's miracle mile, April 1935. It would be wide-bodied jets traveling this same route that would turn Waikiki into a Mecca for the masses after World War II.

4. "Lucky you come Hawai'i," locals say to anyone in the Islands. To tandem surfers they say, "Lucky you come Hawai'i *now*, not *then*." In ancient times surfing was not only the "sport of kings," certain surfing sites were *kapu*, reserved exclusively for chiefs and chiefesses. And forget about tandem surfing anywhere if you were not of the *ali'i* class, for tandem surfing was *kapu*. The penalty for *kapu* violation — death.[11]

5. Seven of Hawai'i's acclaimed beach boys. Noted not only for surfing, canoeing, life-saving, swimming, and teaching abilities, they were also expected to play the *'ukulele* and sing. Big boards were the norm as were colorful names (left to right): Charles Soupy Coelho; Blue Makua; Turkey Love; David P. Kahanamoku, the beach boys' captain; Ox Keaulani; Curly Cornwell; and Louis Kahanamoku.

On a calm December 7, 1941, the Japanese struck with complete surprise, having sent a task force of thirty-one ships undetected across the North Pacific. From four aircraft carriers, the first of 360 aircraft crossed the northern coast of Oʻahu at 7:55 A.M. and began a devastating attack. A second wave followed, aimed at military bases across the Island. When the attack was completed, 21 ships in Pearl Harbor were sunk or heavily damaged, 92 navy planes were lost and 31 damaged, and the army air corps lost 96 and had 128 damaged. The attacking force lost 55 airplanes and 5 midget submarines. While 64 Japanese were killed and 1 captured, 2,390 Americans were killed and 1,178 were wounded.

Among the dead on Oʻahu were 49 civilians, many of them killed by American shells that fell short of attacking aircraft. It was Hawaiʻi's first taste of what World War II was to mean, but it was by no means the last. On the very day of the attack, military censors went to work. Restrictions were put on newspapers, magazines, and radio broadcasts. In a matter of hours, the military declared martial law throughout the Islands, and Lieutenant General Walter Short declared himself the "military governor" of Hawaiʻi. Martial law lasted far longer than it should have. In 1942 the territory's governor, Ingram Stainback, and its attorney general, J. Garner Anthony, went to Washington to ask the secretary of the interior, Harold Ickes, for help. Through Ickes's influence many of the martial law restrictions were eased, but it was not until October 24, 1944, that President Franklin D. Roosevelt abolished martial law in the Islands. Hawaiʻi residents could breathe easier, freed from many annoying and often unnecessary restrictions.

Left: The ammunition magazine of the USS *Shaw* explodes, cutting the ship in half. The near half would stay afloat and later be reconstructed.
Spread: Ford Island — view from a camera aboard a Japanese plane as it makes a diving attack on Ford Island and Battleship Row, Pearl Harbor, December 7, 1941.

Below: The battleship USS *Arizona* burns furiously after sustaining a direct hit, exploding stored ammunition — 1,177 sailors and marines perish.

Ford Island — view from the ground near Hanger 6, as crewmen watch the devastation around them and along Battleship Row.

Volunteer civilian women engaged in vital, top secret work for the U.S. Army. "The least known of the women's uniformed services," the Women's Air Raid Defense (WARD) had the "responsibility of plotting and evaluating radar reports on all air and surface craft for the Hawaiian Islands area"[12] throughout World War II. They numbered in the hundreds, in units on various islands. Not even their families knew the nature of their assignment or even where they worked. Recruited primarily from Island residents, when demand exceeded available supply, some recruiting was done — with great secrecy — on the Mainland.

In addition to the mail censorship, long-distance telephone calls were subject to censorship. All calls had to be in English so an eavesdropping censor could understand all that was being said. Callers could not discuss the weather, among other topics. Long lines for some goods became commonplace. Because of gas rationing, buses were crowded with servicemen jostling civilians for space. Liquor also was rationed. Fresh eggs were hard to come by, as was meat. Home victory gardens sprouted, with one estimate putting them at fifteen thousand by August 1942, and thirteen community gardens were cultivated in parks and vacant lots.

Labor shortages became acute with men away in service. Women filled many jobs, including some that they had been denied before, such as driving trucks and other heavy equipment and even repairing them. Some became welders, while others worked at aircraft maintenance.

Trenches and shelters were constructed throughout Oʻahu, and air-raid drills were held. There seemed to be little doubt that the Japanese would attack again, but as the months went by the skies over Hawaiʻi remained clear except for a two-aircraft Japanese reconnaissance flight on March 4, 1942. The flight ran into heavy cloud cover, and one aircraft dropped its bombs out to sea while the other dropped them on an undeveloped area of Tantalus, a hilly area behind the city proper.

The Matsujiro Otanis, one family among 160,000 Japanese in Hawai'i (37 percent of the population, compared to 25 percent Caucasian), as of December 7, 1941. In this photo the time is 1943, and matriarch Kane Otani; eldest son Jiroichi; his wife, Elsie; and son Kenji gather in front of their hard-won Mānoa Valley home (purchased in 1940 against objections by Caucasian neighbors) to commemorate Kenji's departure to serve in the U.S. Army. Kane would send four of five sons off to military service. One son, Jay, remained at home. Days, he operated the family business importing essential foods for military and civilian populations. Evenings, he worked for the Honolulu Police Department as a curfew warden and also undercover — even from his family — for military intelligence. Absent from the photo, and the family, was patriarch Matsujiro. While at home on the evening of December 7, he was seized and incarcerated as a Japanese enemy alien for the duration of the war.

Volunteers, also, were the 2,686 Hawai'i Americans of Japanese Ancestry (AJAs) who were accepted to form the 442d Infantry Regimental Combat Team in the spring of 1943 and who gathered at 'Iolani Palace in a historical send-off. As a segregated unit they distinguished themselves in Italy and France, becoming the most decorated unit — for its size — in American history. Over half a century later one of its surviving members, Edward M. Yamasaki, wrote:
"I believe (their) major contribution lies in their having helped make America a better, richer place in which to live for everyone; we have seen appreciable increase in sensitivity to the rights of all its citizens, including minorities, and in offering of equal opportunities in education, the arts, politics and business."[13]

Below: Not all the Hawai'i wartime military action was on O'ahu. On Maui, Frankie and Johnnie's Lunch Counter and accessory shoe shine boys attracted off-duty soldiers and sailors.

Three sailors get a *hula* lesson from the famous comedienne, "Hilo Hattie," Clara Melekahaili Baxter Douglas Inter Nelson, who taught school for 20 years before singing and dancing her way into the hearts of audiences in Hawai'i and on the Mainland, with such comic numbers as "The Cockeyed Mayor of Kaunakakai" and "When Hilo Hattie Does the Hilo Hop."

In the city, some buildings were painted in camouflage colors. The Honolulu Academy of Arts and the Bishop Museum moved valuable works to safer places. Soldiers and sailors—and some civilian helpers—strung barbed wire on vulnerable beaches. Honolulu was divided into two evacuation zones by the Office of Civil Defense, and instructions were issued concerning what to carry if one had to evacuate. Women and children were to be the evacuees, while males over fifteen years of age were to stay to fight fires. The military took over half the public parks on O'ahu for storage sites; schools were seized; and sugar and pineapple plantations gave up land, equipment, and men. One historian notes that more than three hundred thousand acres of land were occupied by the military in Hawai'i during the war years. Curfew and blackouts were enforced vigorously, and everyone over the age

of six had to be fingerprinted and carry an identification card.

The young American men who came to Hawai'i during the war years were as varied as the nation they came from, and military-civilian liaisons took place in places ranging from houses of prostitution to the homes of wealthy and influential Islanders. The war lent an urgency to romances. Many of the men stationed briefly in Hawai'i went on into the Pacific, some never to return. It was a time when hearts were broken in the bittersweet atmosphere of the conflict and the Islands. It was clear that Hawai'i would never be quite the same.

For the Japanese in the Islands, it certainly would never be the same. At first denied the opportunity to serve, young Japanese males did whatever they could for the

V-J Day in Honolulu. Finally, after four days of high-intensity expectation and false reports — including a two-hour celebration on August 12 — official confirmation of victory arrived at 1:42 P.M., August 14, 1945. Jubilant pandemonium followed. The city celebrated for two days and, again, on September 2 — the official V-J Day when the Japanese formally surrendered aboard the USS *Missouri* in Tokyo Bay — with the Honolulu Victory Parade.[14]

The city erupted with relief — and somber reflection.

war effort until the military finally allowed them to volunteer. Some were already in the Hawai'i National Guard, and when they were forced out due to their race, some formed the Varsity Victory Volunteers. They eventually segued into units, which were designated the 100th Battalion and the 442d Regimental Combat Team, and went on to win glory and suffer high casualty rates in Europe, becoming the most decorated unit in the American army. It was the Japanese way of proving a point. They continued to prove it after the war—the veterans went to college on the G.I. Bill and returned to the Islands to move swiftly and decisively into powerful political positions. Never again did anyone question their patriotism or their rights to whatever political, economic, or social positions to which they would aspire.

Volcano!

The give and take of nature is nowhere more clearly or impressively illustrated than in Hawai'i's dynamic vulcanism. In the photos here of Mauna Loa's April 1926 eruption we see almost simultaneous destruction and creation.

Hawaiians of old developed a body of wonderfully creative legends and *mele* about the phenomenon, giving evidence of their knowledge that the Hawai'i archipelago was formed by volcanic action in a specific sequence. It is noteworthy that Pele, the volcano goddess, "greatly loved in spite of her bad temper," was known as *Pele-honua-mea* (Pele-the-sacred-earth-person).[15]

While all of Hawai'i's Islands are of volcanic origin, the volcanoes of the Island of Hawai'i (the youngest of the Islands) include two of the world's most active — Mauna Loa and Kīlauea. The Island as a whole represents the coalescence of five volcanoes; Kohala Volcano is the oldest, revealing the greatest erosion. The dormant Mauna Kea erupted last about 4,500 years ago. Still considered active, Hualālai erupts at about 250-year intervals, the most recent being 1801. Mauna Loa is expected to erupt frequently throughout the foreseeable future.[16] As of June 2002, Kīlauea, Hawai'i Island's youngest emerged volcano, continues in an eruption that began January 3, 1983 — while deep under the sea off the southern coast of Hawai'i, Lō'ihi Volcano slowly builds a mass above the floor of the sea, preparing to emerge as Hawai'i's newest island, in about 60,000 years.

1. Eruption of Mauna Loa advancing on Ho'ōpūloa Landing; height of flow — 50 feet; width — 1,500 feet. April 19, 1926.

2. Alexander P. Lancaster, billed as the "first guide to the volcano," takes a break in his duties at Kīlauea Crater. Records identify him as one-half Native American (Cherokee) and one-half African American.

3. Slow moving is this fiery avalanche of lava — note man at right, between car and flow. April 18, 1926, Mauna Loa eruption.

4. River of molten lava as it joins the sea at the village of Ho'ōpūloa, Hawai'i; 6:20 A.M., April 18, 1926. Note structure visible in flow.

3. THE HUGE WAVE OF A-A LAVA CREPT ACROSS THE HOOPULOA ROAD AFTER DESTRUCTION OF THE HAWAIIAN VILLAGE APRIL 18 1926

4. RIVER OF MOLTEN LAVA AS IT JOINS THE SEA AT THE VILLAGE OF HOOPULOA OF HAWAII AT 6:21 A.M. APRIL 18

Tsunami!

2.

1.

Hawaiians call them *kaie'e* or *hō'e'e*. In English, the long-standing but inaccurate descriptive phrase is "tidal wave." The internationally accepted designation is the Japanese word *tsunami* (harbor wave) to label a series of rapidly moving ocean waves generated by:

1. the sudden rise or fall of a section of Earth's crust below or near the ocean (earthquake);

2. volcanic activity; or

3. a landslide occurring below or above the ocean surface.

These seismic sea waves have extremely long wavelengths and may travel thousands of miles at speeds of a jet plane. As they approach shallower waters near shorelines, they slow down, resulting in an increase in wave height and destructive power. Though a *tsunami* is imperceptible in the open ocean, the shore onslaught is sudden and without warning, save for receding waters immediately preceding the first wave. On shore, the deluge — which may arrive at speeds around 30 miles per hour — is perceived not as a breaking wave but as a series of surges, typically arriving 5 to 15 minutes apart. Usually "the third or fourth wave is the highest, with ten or more significant waves arriving over a period of several hours."[17] This out-of-bounds sea may strike at heights exceeding 30 feet and may travel inland for a mile or more.

Hawai'i is exposed to *tsunamis* generated around the Pacific Ocean's fault zones known as the "Rim of Fire." On record since the first recorded *tsunami* to strike Hawai'i (1819, leading to 46 fatalities) is a total of 86 events, 15 causing moderate or greater damage. In addition to locally generated disturbances, waves reaching Hawai'i have originated in South America, Kamchatka, and the Aleutian Islands.

Historically, Hilo — on the Big Island of Hawai'i — has been distressingly vulnerable. On April 1, 1946, a *tsunami* generated in the Aleutian Islands arrived without warning as a series of three waves, reportedly of heights up to 35 feet above sea level, causing 83 deaths.

From Chile, in 1960, Hilo received a second massively destructive hit. The surge made contact at speeds reported to be as great as 40 miles per hour in heights up to 35 feet. Lives lost — 61.

Using technology brought to the fore during World War II, a warning system was developed and is now in place under the direction of the Pacific Tsunami Warning Center of the National Oceanic and Atmospheric Administration at 'Ewa Beach on O'ahu, serving Hawai'i and 25 countries of the Pacific Rim.

1. Coming ashore like a massive, high-speed rising tide, the wave engulfs Pu'umaile Hospital grounds, Hilo, April 1, 1946.

2. The waterfront at Hilo, on Hawai'i Island, sustained the heaviest damage of the April 1, 1946, *tsunami*. Hilo lost 83 lives.

3. On Kaua'i, April 1, 1946, property damage included the taro farm of this couple.

4. Inundation at Kahuku, on O'ahu's northern shore, in the aftermath of the April 1, 1946, *tsunami*.

5. Waters of the April 1, 1946, *tsunami* surround the Joseph Kenewa residence at Kahului — on Maui.

6. Kamehameha Avenue, downtown Hilo, April 1, 1946. After Hilo cleaned up and rebuilt, the city would be hit by an equally devastating *tsunami* in 1960.

A Rich Tradition

What Anna Rice Cooke, a Hawai'i-born daughter of New England missionaries, said in 1927 about the purpose of her legacy in founding the Honolulu Academy of Arts also epitomizes the mission of numerous other art-related organizations that together form a strong community-wide support base for the arts. In her words:

… That our children of many nationalities and races, born far from the centers of art, may receive an intimation of their own cultural legacy and wake to the ideals embodied in the arts of their neighbors … may perceive a foundation on which a new culture, enriched by the old strains, may be built in these islands.

Following a visit to the Academy's opening in 1927, Shao Chang Lee of the University of Hawai'i's Chinese language and history department expressed his appraisal in a note to Mrs. Cook: *The whole treasure house is a symbol of beauty, harmony and peace. It is educational and full of inspiration. Intellectually and spiritually, Hawai'i is made richer by your wonderful gift. It is a blessing to the people and a benediction to the world.*[18]

1. Honolulu Theatre for Youth, nearing its first half-century mark, features the best of contemporary children's theatre. Its extraordinary work brings continuing recognition worldwide.

2. "Two Nudes on a Tahitian Beach," by Paul Gauguin, 1894, a work selected in 1931 for the Honolulu Academy of Arts by founder Anna Rice Cooke, before Gauguin was well known.[19]

3. "The Chief's Canoe," fresco section by Jean Charlot. Arriving in 1949 to teach at the University of Hawai'i, the Paris-born artist Jean Charlot (1898–1979) made Hawai'i his home base the rest of his life. A Fellow in Perpetuity of the Metropolitan Museum of Art, Charlot earned international acclaim for a bold, sculptural style developed while working with Diego Rivera in Mexico. His monumental frescoes of Hawaiian subject matter won plaudits at home.

4. Lorraine Dove, as Nellie Forbush, delighted Honolulu Community Theatre audiences in the 1955 production of *South Pacific*, playing 39 performances in Honolulu at Ruger Theater and then on tour to six U.S. armed forces bases in the Pacific.

5. The Honolulu Symphony, one of the community's fine cultural resources since 1900, is now a professional orchestra featuring guest artists of the highest renown. The Symphony is especially proud of its Youth Series for schoolchildren.

6. Madge Tennent drawing. Madge Tennent (1889–1972), an English-born art prodigy schooled at The Academie Julien in Paris, turned a Honolulu stopover into half a century of interpreting the "aesthetic" of the Hawaiian people. "Even if the Hawaiians were to vanish as a race they would live forever in the paintings of Madge Tennent," says John Dominis Holt, part-Hawaiian scholar.

7. With a founding date of 1915, Diamond Head Theatre (formerly Footlights Club, then Honolulu Community Theatre) is one of the oldest community theatres in the United States. It is often granted first nonprofessional production rights. Dress rehearsal, *Carousel*, 1958.

2.

3.

4.

6.

7.

Making Music

1. In the 1930s and 1940s — pre-TV days — the radio program "Hawai'i Calls" contributed greatly to popularizing Hawaiian music, when it was heard globally by millions via shortwave. Webley Edwards (left), Harry Owens (right).

2 . A feeling of *'ohana* prevails in this typical garage practice session of the *Leo Nahenahe* Singers and the Sometime Group, c. 1970s (left to right): Noelani Kanoho Mahoe, Mona Noelani Teves, Lynette Kaopuiki Paglinawan, Ethelynne Kaleimokihana Teves, Clarence Hohu, Albert Kaailau, Bobby Ayeres, Harold Hakuole, and Francis Hookano.

3. The first all–slack key album featured the late Leonard Kwan (Tradewinds Records), whose style influenced many later *ki hō'alu* artists.

4. Singing along together for 71 years, "Alex" and Peggy Anderson, two musically gifted *keiki o ka 'āina* (children of the land). She was a protégé of opera star Nellie Melba and he was a successful businessman, whose memorable Hawaiian songs made him the leading *hapa-haole* (part-white, part-Hawaiian) Island composer for many years from the 1920s to the 1970s.[20]

5. The Kamehameha Schools Song Contest is held annually at Neal Blaisdell Center arena, where it is seen and broadcast live on radio, television, and live streaming video.

6. Savor it and save it. Mid-20th century, *malihini* (newcomer) Margaret Williams started recording music she heard on the beaches and at backyard parties, feeling few were paying attention to the local style and that it should not be lost. Thus began Tradewinds Records.

7. Mākaha Sons of Ni'ihau, 1982. With 19 albums, 20 *Hoku* Awards, and critical acclaim for "exquisiteness" and virtuosity, the Mākaha Sons are all about traditional Hawaiian sounds. And to founder Louis "Moon" Kauakahi that means Hawaiian language, guitars, upright bass, *'ukulele,* and an undefinable something Moon can't explain, but it has to do with "sticking with the roots." It's a positive approach, to sing the song that describes "the Hawaiian people as flowers who will live, who will continue to survive …"[21]

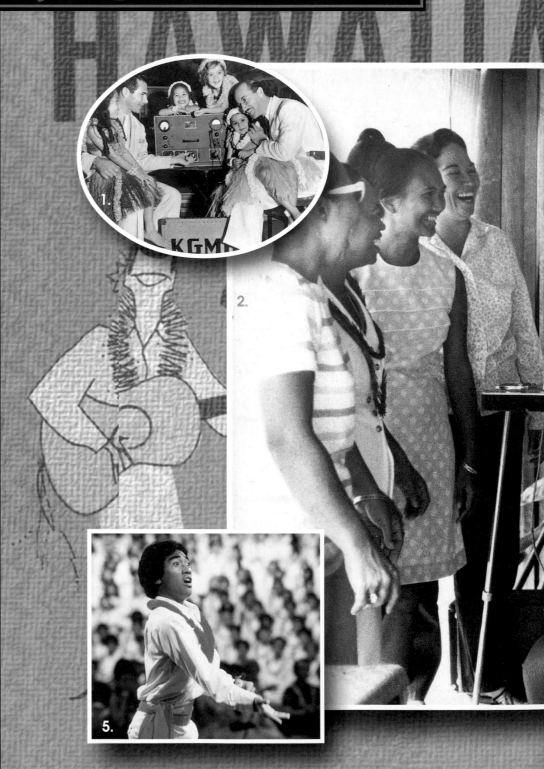

STYLE

3.

4.

6. PARTY SONGS
HAWAIIAN STYLE

FEATURING HAWAII'S OWN SLACK KEY GUITAR
WITH LEONARD KWAN...A TRADEWINDS RECORD

7.

Stumping for Hawai'i
statehood as the 49th
state, the Hawai'i
Statehood Commission
and the Hawai'i
Visitors Bureau entered
this float in the 1949
Inaugural Parade,
Washington, D.C.

HAWAII
THE 49TH STATE

HAWAII the 49th STATE

Chapter 5

The end of the war was like the opening of a door onto a new era. The veterans of the 100th Battalion and 442d Regimental Combat Team, and the other units in which Americans of Japanese ancestry had served so well, were inclined to change the political posture of the Islands; and in 1954 they did. That was the year of the great political revolution that saw most of the old Republican power elite turned out of office and a new Democratic party power elite move in.

Two of Hawai'i's biggest — and brightest — boosters: the Islands' celebrated Olympic swimming champion, Duke Kahanamoku, and affable radio and television star of the '50s, Arthur Godfrey, who contributed to a revival of interest in the 'ukulele.

Left: Three laborers at work on an irrigation ditch, ʻEwa Plantation, Oʻahu. Above: Philip P. Maxwell (left), Employers Council president, with labor leader Jack Hall (right), 1964, 20th anniversary year of Hawaiʻi sugar workers.

The new focus gave rise to a concomitant demand for statehood, as more and more people demanded greater representation.

Territorial status suddenly was not enough. The governor of Hawaiʻi was not an elected official, chosen by the people of the Islands, but a political appointee. Islanders could send a delegate to Congress, but the delegate could not vote. Congress retained the power to establish or abolish legislative positions in Hawaiʻi and could, if it wished, even abolish the territorial government. The implication was that the people of the Islands were not capable of making their own informed decisions, and there was, as well, a strong hint of racism, with some southern congressmen looking askance at Hawaiʻi's brown and mixed races.

For the establishment in Hawaiʻi, change meant a certain amount of risk. They were joined in apprehension by some Hawaiians and by some of the old *kamaʻāina* (native) elite, whose memories were, perhaps, of a more gracious time. Still, most Islanders favored statehood, as did the territorial legislature and the me-

dia. The labor unions came in for a great deal of scrutiny, particularly the International Longshoremen's and Warehousemen's Union (ILWU). The ILWU was the largest, most controversial, best-led, and most militant union in Hawaiʻi, and it often was accused of harboring Communists. Its charismatic leader was Jack Wayne Hall, a brilliant, hard-drinking, hardworking, and pragmatic man. The unions, and especially the ILWU, became a force in Island life, and they were often an irritant to businessmen and politicians.

The specter of communism began to fade from the unions at the same time as the thrust for statehood was rising. One of the factors that brought about greater acceptance of the unions was the fact that many members of the ILWU had joined other Hawaiʻi men in going off to Korea to fight the Communists. Meanwhile, Hawaiʻi's strategy shifted from coupling Alaska and Hawaiʻi statehood concerns to allowing Alaska to become a state first; the rationale was that once Congress accepted Alaska it could not then deny Hawaiʻi. This proved to be true. In May 1958 the Alaska statehood bill

On February 10, 1954, in a daylong rally downtown on Bishop Street in Honolulu 116,000 Hawai'i residents signed the "Statehood Honor Roll" petitioning Congress for statehood. The effort achieved publicity but not statehood.

1843   1883   1893

1896   1900   1959

Hawai'i's coat of arms had its beginnings in 1842, when Kamehameha III sent representatives abroad to negotiate treaties to guarantee Hawai'i's continued independence and, further, to seek professionals about design of a royal seal or crest. The first version was prepared by Herald's College, London. The version adopted in 1845 served with little modification throughout the monarchy and remains the basis for the statehood seal.[1] (Left to right, top row) Coat of Arms, Hawaiian monarchy, London, 1843–1844; Coat of Arms, 1883 (King Kalākaua's coronation invitation); Great Seal, Republic of Hawai'i, 1893; (bottom row, left to right) Transitional Seal, provisional government, 1896; Territorial Seal, 1900; Coat of Arms, State of Hawai'i, 1959.

passed the House, in June it passed the Senate. Alaska became the forty-ninth state, and Hawai'i began its all-out push for statehood.

In February 1959 the House Committee on Interior and Insular Affairs voted favorably for Hawai'i statehood, and the Senate followed suit in March. On March 11, 1959, the Senate passed the statehood bill, and the following morning the full House of Representatives also passed it. On March 12 there was an air of expectancy in Hawai'i. Then the news flashed that Hawai'i was—at long last—the fiftieth state.

Church bells began to peal all over the city. People poured out of buildings and into the streets to greet one another as fully represented United States citizens. Civil defense sirens sounded. Newspapers began preparing extra editions. That night there were bonfires on the beaches that knew the footprints of the old Polynesian voyagers. Some groups gathered in churches to hear ministers invoke God's blessings on this newest state. Bartenders were busy, which meant police were busy not in making arrests but in trying to see that people were not hurt. There was a general mood of euphoria.

But not for all. There were a few—and perhaps only a few—who looked back in time and recalled the old, colorful, vibrant society that had existed in the not-too-dim past. They remembered their history before the coming of the tall ships with their strangers from strange lands. They felt that in a sense the advent of statehood bound them closer to a brash young nation and carried them farther from their beginnings. These few looked out and wept.

The statehood boom changed the face of Hawai'i in dramatic ways. Now the Islands were split into four counties. The city limits of Honolulu stretched to encompass the Islands at the northwest end of the chain—sixteen hundred miles of islands, shoals, rocks, and sandbars. Honolulu gave birth to numerous high-rises in the Mainland style, right down to the air-conditioning and the closed windows that shut out the trade winds. Freeways began their sinuous weave across O'ahu.

Statehood strategies continued, with this well-planned photo op for the statehood delegation as it prepared to leave for Washington. (Left to right) Hawai'i Chief Justice E. A. Towse; Hawai'i Senate President Wilfred C. Tsukiyama; Hawai'i Governor Samuel Wilder King; U. S. Congressman Hiram L. Fong.

More green space was covered by concrete, and the population rocketed skyward, from around two hundred fifty thousand in the mid-1950s to more than a million by 1990.

There were positive developments amid the building boom. The East-West Center for Technical and Cultural Interchange became a reality instead of a dream and attracted scholars from all over the world. The University of Hawai'i took on more autonomy even as it grew in stature and numbers. Heightened competition meant that local business began to diversify. Tourism continued to grow and to be the engine that drove the local economy. Honolulu boasted a zoo, a symphony, an opera season, a famous museum, and an art academy. The neighbor Islands began to blossom as tourism increased in places that had been somnolent—some say underdeveloped—and opulent resorts sprang up on the dark lava coastlines.

Slowly, but with a kind of gentle certainty, high-tech industries began to find their way to the Islands. Maui developed an extensive high-tech park. Industries that could segue into high-tech operations began to do so, receiving grants along the way and proving that such technology could work well in the Islands. Satellites linked Hawai'i with major cities around the world, and if some of the romance of Hawai'i was gone, some of the modern advantages had arrived.

In downtown Honolulu, *kama'āina* businessmen who had at first reacted badly to the infusion of Mainland ideas and Mainland capital now began to take advantage of the technology and the rush of new prospects. Many of the old guard retired or were replaced, and a new and adventurous spirit seized the business community so that Honolulu firms could

Their smiles belie reality, as statehood was not yet a done deal in July 1958, when the statehood delegation included (left to right): former Hawai'i Governor Oren E. Long; Delegate to Congress Mrs. Joseph R. Farrington; last appointed Hawai'i Governor William F. Quinn; Samuel W. King; and Lorrin P. Thurston, chairman, Hawai'i Statehood Commission.

begin to export ideas and services. Honolulu-trained technicians turned up in many exotic parts of the world, particularly in places where sugar and pineapple were grown. Some business leaders found that Hawai'i's mid-Pacific location, with its favorable time zone, could be an asset in dealing with the economies of Asia as well as the Mainland. The Islands became a linkage point and all at once began to live up to their nickname as the Crossroads of the Pacific.

In the midst of all this the ordinary people of Hawai'i—the farmers and fishermen, the housewives and shopkeepers, the construction workers and flower growers—all came to grips with the new ways and the new economy. They went about their business with aplomb, enjoying the world's greatest climate even as they had to work hard to maintain a decent standard of living in one of the world's most expensive places. The Islands grew to have the highest percentage of working wives in the nation. Taxes were among the highest, and it was a fortunate couple who could afford to buy a home. The land knew droughts and the economy knew recessions, sugar and pineapple industries declined, but it would have been difficult to find Hawai'i citizens who would willingly live elsewhere. Partly it was the climate that held them, partly the strong sense of family, and partly the beauty of sun-washed lands in a cerulean sea under a vaulting sky.

It would be March 12, 1959, before the U.S. Congress passed the bill, making Hawai'i statehood a reality. President Eisenhower designated August 21 as Admission Day, when, in Honolulu, the Royal Hawaiian Band marks the occasion at 'Iolani Palace, once again the coming-together site for a historic status-changing event.

A Vibrant Community

1. Democrat parade profile, June 1963 — President John F. Kennedy; Hawai'i Governor (and statehood architect) John A. Burns; highly decorated 442d Regimental Combat Team veteran and U.S. Senator Daniel K. Inouye.

2. Lt. Governor John D. Waihe'e, 1982, became Hawai'i's first elected governor of Hawaiian descent in 1986.

3. Myron B. "Pinky" Thompson, 1924–2001. Called "a lion in service to his fellow Hawaiians and an icon in the renaissance of that native culture,"[2] his areas of leadership centered around education, health, social services, and land use.

4. Gladys Ainoa Brandt — education and community affairs leader; chairwoman emeritus, Board of Regents, University of Hawai'i, 2002.

5. Side by side — at the 1978 rededication ceremonies, 'Iolani Palace — family members of Hawai'i's last reigning monarch, *maka'āinana* (commoners), Asian Americans, and others (left to right): Edward Kawananakoa; the Reverend Abraham K. Akaka; *kumu hula* 'Iolani Luahine; Abigail Kekaulike Kawananakoa; Governor George R. Ariyoshi; two unidentified women; Regina Kawananakoa; unidentified man.

6. Governor George R. Ariyoshi, Hawai'i's first governor of Japanese ancestry, signs Festival of Trees Day proclamation, November 30, 1979, with members of The Queen's Medical Center Auxiliary and Queen's President Will J. Henderson.

7. John D. Bellinger, 1986, leader in community affairs and banking sector — he was with First Hawaiian Bank for 47 years.

8. John W. A. "Doc" Buyers took the helm of C. Brewer and Company — Hawai'i's oldest company — 1975.

9. Governor Benjamin J. Cayetano — Hawai'i's first governor of Filipino ancestry, 1994–2002.

10. Kaua'i-born U.S. Senator Spark M. Matsunaga was a Harvard graduate and another highly decorated 442d Regiment veteran; he also worked tirelessly in community affairs. His special mission — peace. La Pietra, Hawai'i School for Girls, December 1982.

In the second half of the 20th century, several factors converged to result in a spectacular building boom and the transformation of Honolulu from a laid-back agrarian territorial outpost (with sugar, pineapple, and the federal government sustaining the Islands' economy) to the metropolitan center of a world-renowned visitor destination area. Pent-up demand for construction following four years of no construction during World War II, increased awareness of the Islands, and a burgeoning middle class ripe for travel all contributed to the phenomenon. Then, in 1959, Hawai'i was granted statehood, and the first jet flights to Hawai'i were inaugurated, bringing more visitors than there were hotel rooms. Five airlines complained they were turning away bookings for lack of rooms. When Pan Am's Willis G. Lipscomb predicted, "You have a tourist industry that could come from obscurity to eclipse all other industries in Hawai'i," it sounded less than realistic. Yet, it was the future.[3]

1. In the spirit of the times — Windward City Shopping Center, an exuberant celebration of Hawaiian motifs, 1959.

2. Native son Chinn Ho, founder of Capital Investment Co. and one of O'ahu's most dominant developers, built the 'Ilikai Hotel, 1964, and bought 9,000 acres of leeward coastland to develop Mākaha Resort, 1969.

3. "The state bird" was jokingly identified as the construction crane, so numerous were they during the '60s and '70s. This "bird" works on the site of the Hawai'i State Capitol, completed 1968.

4. Ala Moana Shopping Center's Phase Two, under construction, 1966 (Phase One was completed in 1959) — when complete it would be billed as the "world's largest modern shopping center."

5. Industrialist Henry J. Kaiser, one of the earliest of the big developers, thought expansively and moved with lightning speed, leaving a legacy of hotel, residential, and commercial projects: in Waikīkī — Hilton Hawaiian Village; in East O'ahu — 6,000 richly developed suburban acres now known as Hawai'i–Kai.

6. Waikīkī — the 1 1/2-mile-long concrete crescent that keeps Hawai'i's visitor industry vibrant. It's the state's top industry.

7. Developer Christopher B. Hemmeter with business partner Diane Plotts and architect George Whisenand watching the installation of an Edward Brownlee sculpture at Hemmeter's new Hyatt Regency Waikīkī, 1976.

8. Edward Brownlee's hanging sculpture at the Hyatt Regency Hotel in Waikīkī.

9. Gateway to Waikīkī — the award-winning Hawai'i Convention Center, its fabric sails a metaphor for the sails of ancient voyaging canoes, establishing the Islands as the place of the "people of the canoe."

5.

6.

7.

8.

9.

©Monte Costa

A True Melting Pot

4.

7.

The faces of Hawai'i's youth speak volumes about the people of the Islands and, in their beauty, evoke a wisdom that intellect sometimes overlooks.

Endlessly fascinating, these faces reflecting the blending of diverse people comprise a kaleidoscopically variable garden — beauty enjoyable for itself alone, priceless for its lesson unspoken.

1. A dancer's moment of quiet before a performance — Aloha Week Festival, Royal Court Investiture, Hawai'i State Capitol, September 6, 1974.

2. Riveted attention — Hawaiian warrior, Aloha Week Court, September 19, 1974.

3. Spectator — the first Duke Kahanamoku Outrigger Canoe Regatta, August 10, 1974.

4. Smiles — St. Clement's School, October 1982.

5. Shared information — nursery school, March 1971.

6. Jubilant chorus — Punahou and Kaiser High School pep squads, January 9, 1982.

7. Hula sparkle — Kapi'olani Park, October 1975.

Mostly what has kept Hawaiian citizens in the Islands is the miracle of mixing, the wonderful melding of races that in turn generates the great tolerance for one another and the appreciation of other cultures and customs. It is true that there are occasional racial incidents; with a population of more than a million there will be such aberrations. But in a real sense the intermarriages and the mixing of diverse races have made for a populace that enjoys the differences among its neighbors.

This is the second of the great epics of Hawai'i, following in the wake of the first great epic of the Polynesian voyages of discovery and colonization. When they stood in the graceful double-hulled canoes and looked on the new land at the apex of the Polynesian Triangle, those old voyagers had no inkling of the civilization that would spring from their discovery. They knew they had found a strange new land replete with phenomena unknown to them—snow and erupting volcanoes—but it was beyond their knowledge and abilities to foresee what the land would generate. They might have been gratified to sense that the Islands one day would be more than a beauteous and busy mid-ocean crossroads; they would be a model for a world in which racial equality and racial acceptance is a prerequisite for world peace.

All photos: ©Monte Costa

Youth of Hawai'i
learning the ropes
for their voyage
through life — together.
Inset: *Hōkūle'a*
outward bound!
E Ola Mau ...
To Thrive Always.

Voyaging

HOLDS OUR PAST AND FUTURE

At the 25th anniversary of the launching of the voyaging canoe *Hōkūle'a*, April 2000, the late Myron B. Thompson, then president of the Polynesian Voyaging Society (PVS), emphasized that PVS is about the present and the future as well as the past, the validation and celebration of the accomplishments of the ancient Polynesian voyagers. He set the navigational direction for the 21st century as "Mālama Hawai'i: Navigating the Future" — take care of Hawai'i and her people, that they may thrive always. Following are excerpts from his message:

Hōkūle'a has now sailed more than 100,000 miles. We have traveled to every point in the vast Polynesian Triangle, reunifying kin and celebrating our shared voyaging heritage. Our canoe family has even grown to include the native people of Alaska. Our educational programs have reached more than half a million students across the state.

Our canoe family is large and knows no ethnic or economic boundaries — we are bound together by our deep love of Hawai'i and our commitment of ensuring that the Hawai'i we know and love today is a place worthy of leaving to our children and those that will follow them. Our Malama Hawai'i vision is that Hawai'i, our island home, be a place where the land and sea are cared for and communities are healthy and safe for all people.

(continued on page 114)

1. The voyaging canoe *Hawai'i Loa* off the island of Moloka'i, 1995. The double canoe was made from two Sitka spruce logs from Alaska. In 1973 there were no Polynesian voyaging canoes; in 2000, there were six with others under construction.

2. "With the backlight of the rising sun, you read the face of the sea ... Without the moon, the only way you can navigate in the middle of the day is by the direction of the waves."[4]
—Nainoa Thompson, master navigator

3. The history-making voyaging canoe *Hōkūle'a* in the Kaiwi Channel between O'ahu and Moloka'i.

4. Strong hands lashing *'iako* (cross beams) of the *Hawai'i Loa* with sennit, which provides strength and flexibility to a canoe's critical stress points.[5]

5. The welcoming of *Hōkūle'a* on her return home from her historic voyage to Tahiti, 1976, off Waikīkī.

6. Restoration of the revered *Hōkūle'a* elicits the recall of the visionaries who gave her life, ushering in a new era of Polynesian accomplishment — Polynesian Voyaging Society cofounders scholar Ben Finney; waterman Tommy Holmes; artist Herb Kane; Caroline Islander navigator Mau Piailug; scientist Will Kyselka; and community leader/*makua*-in-fact Myron B. Thompson, who provided the information, support, and inspiration Nainoa Thompson needed to become Hawai'i's first modern master navigator.

All photos this page: ©Monte Costa

3.

4.

6.

1.

2.

Myron Thompson's vision for the voyage ahead had, in fact, already begun. One example among many: PVS, in conjunction with Wai'anae High School Marine Science Learning Center, presented a two-year program, "Ho'olōkāhi: Charting a Course for Life," which was designed to teach youngsters how to chart a course for their lives as they worked together to solve problems.[6] The program took students out of classrooms and put them into their own aquaculture farm and aboard a voyaging canoe, to illustrate practical applications for classroom learning.

The work was an integration of "lessons in oceanography, meteorology, astronomy, geography and the cultural heritage of various regions of the island, and (taught) students self-reliance."[7]

The vision continues to unfold. In 2002 PVS, in partnership with the Department of Education, the University of Hawai'i, and other educational and community partnerships, presented an Ocean Learning Program for high school students, in which the curriculum integrated academic requirements with a series of experientially based activities that included traditional navigational skills.

Master navigator and program director Nainoa Thompson defines the skill necessary to learn to navigate by traditional methods — learning to read the stars and the waves and developing the senses — as "inner technology." The navigator trained in traditional skills relies on that inner technology rather than the "outer technology" of high-tech development, and Thompson believes that these skills have application to living in the contemporary world. His mission in passing on the ancient art is more than sentiment about recalling the past. It arises from his conviction that those youngsters who master "inner technology" will lead our technological progress in the right direction.

1. A Tahitian boy welcomes *Hōkūle'a*, Pape'ete, Tahiti Island, 1995.

2. Canoes and community gather, Mākua Valley, at funeral ceremonies of well-loved Hawaiian musician Israel Kamakawiwo'ole, 1997.

3. Ceremonies, 1995, welcoming the *wa'a* (canoes), Taiohae, Nuku Hiva, the Marquesas Islands, quite probably the homeland of Hawai'i's original settlers.[8] What began in 1973 as a scientific experiment to build a replica of a traditional voyaging canoe for a one-time sail to Tahiti, became a catalyst for a generation of cultural renewal and a symbol of the richness of Hawaiian culture and seafaring heritage that links all of the peoples of Polynesia.

4. *'Awa* ceremony for the arrival of *Hōkūle'a* on Maui, during her statewide sail, 1997. The sail to "connect" Hawaiian communities revealed that cultural renewal is, indeed, underway within these communities and that Hawaiians are celebrating the strengths of a culturally and racially diverse people.

All photos this page: ©Monte Costa

AUTHOR: Scott C. S. Stone is the author of 26 previous works, with other works in progress. He is a former correspondent for Reuters, Cox News Service, and the New York Times News Service. One of his novels won the coveted Edgar (comparable to the Oscar for films) for suspense fiction, and a film script was judged as the best travel film script in America. He has lived in Hawai'i since 1958, with extensive travel in Europe, Asia, and Antarctica. He is a retired navy reserve commander who saw combat in the Korean and Vietnam wars. In September 2001, Stone was named writer in residence at the University of Hawai'i in Hilo.

PICTURE EDITOR: Mazeppa King Costa joins Stone for their third collaboration, after *Honolulu, Heart of Hawai'i* and *Otani*. She has a 23-year history of writing for the design profession, during which she became a ghostwriter and author with her own byline. Costa holds degrees from George Washington University and University of Hawai'i. Among her community roles are: former director — Honolulu Theatre for Youth, Hawaiian Music Foundation; former chair — Ethics Commission, City and County, Honolulu; former member — Mayor's Commission on Culture and the Arts.

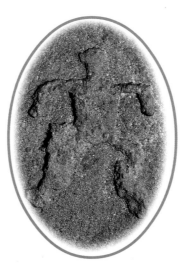

Picture Editor's Acknowledgements

The joy of working on this project was about "the hunt" — for images and information — and "discovery." Even familiar images harbor unfamiliar facts. The finding is the fun. The fun is made possible and greatly enhanced by the people one works with and relies upon — from the project team to the community whose mission it is to preserve and manage Hawai'i's historical resources; from historians, archivists, research specialists, and collectors to Hawaiian language experts, writers and editors, artists, secretaries, lab technicians, graphic designers, and numerous generous people who happen to have a needed photograph or bit of information they are willing to contribute to the work in progress; and the foundation of it all — the photographers.

To the project team — Scott Stone, Micki Fletcher, Danvers Fletcher, DeSoto Brown, Rhoda Hackler, and Jan Stenberg — goes a full measure of appreciation.

Luella Kurkiian, branch chief for historical records, Hawai'i State Archives, and every member of her staff — Jason Achiu, Marlene Donovan, Sandra Harms, Allen Hoof, Patricia Lai, Deborah Lee, Victoria Nihi, and Gina Vergara-Bautista — deserve thanks for their more than a year of assistance.

Outstanding among scores of other helpful contributors were: Judy Bowman, Monte Costa, Page Costa, Tony Costa, Lorraine Dove, Nancy Hedemann, Stuart Ho, Olivier Koning, Jim Manke, Shirley Maxfield, David Montesino, Pepi Nieva, Jay Otani, John Rampage, Mary Richards, Carol Silva, Howard Wolff, Pamela Ho Wong, and David Yamada.

It is a pleasure to acknowledge these institutions, organizations, and firms that in one way or another played a valuable role in the process leading to the completion of this work: Aloha Week Festivals; Bishop Museum; Camera Hawai'i; Diamond Head Theatre; Hawaiian Historical Society; Honolulu Academy of Arts; *The Honolulu Advertiser*; Honolulu Theatre for Youth; Honolulu Symphony; Kamehameha Schools; La Pietra/Hawai'i School for Girls; Library of Hawai'i; Office of the Governor/State of Hawai'i; Office of the President/ University of Hawai'i; Photo Hawai'i; U.S. Army Museum; WATG Architects.

References

Beckwith, Martha Warren. *The Kumulipo: A Hawaiian Creation Chant.* Honolulu: University of Hawai'i Press, 1951.

Bingham, Hiram. *A Residency of Twenty-one Years in the Sandwich Islands.* New York: Praeger, 1969.

Bird, Isabella L. *Six Months in the Sandwich Islands.* Honolulu: University of Hawai'i Press for Friends of the Library of Hawai'i, 1964.

Daggett, the Honorable R. M. Introduction to *King David Kalākaua, Myths and Legends of Hawai'i,* by His Hawaiian Majesty King David Kalākaua. Rutland, V.T., and Tokyo: Charles E. Tuttle Company, 1972.

Ellis, William. *Journal of William Ellis.* Rutland, V.T., and Tokyo: Charles E. Tuttle, 1979.

MacLean, Alistair. *Captain Cook.* Garden City, N.Y.: Doubleday & Company, 1972.

Stone, Scott C. S. *He Mele O Hawai'i.* Los Angeles: Jostens Publishing Group, 1993.

Twain, Mark. *Mark Twain in Hawai'i: Roughing It in the Sandwich Islands.* Foreword by A. Grove Day. Honolulu: Mutual, 1990.

Photo Credits

All photos are from the Hawai'i State Archives unless otherwise noted below.

IHP = Island Heritage Publishing
HHS = Hawaiian Historic Society

Pp. iv - v
©Monte Costa

Pp. x - xi
Mazeppa Costa

Pp. xii - xiii
©Monte Costa

Pp. xvi - 1
IHP - Kozono
Mazeppa Costa (inset)

Pp. 22 - 23
HHS (map)

Pp. 26 - 27
Costa Collection
Derby del. C. Taylor, S.C. (inset)

Pp. 34 - 35
Costa Collection (inset)

Pp. 36 - 37
Costa Collection (images 2, 3, 5, 6)
IHP (images 4, 7, 8, 9)

Pp. 60 - 61
IHP (image 1)

Pp. 62 - 63
Mazeppa Costa (images 2, 5)
Page Costa (image 3)
The Honolulu Advertiser/Monte Costa (images 4, 7)

Costa Collection, The Queen's Medical Center (image 8)
©Monte Costa (image 9)

Pp. 70 - 71
Mazeppa Costa (image 12)

Pp. 78 - 79
Costa Collection (image 7)

Pp. 80 - 81
Costa Collection (images 1, 3)

Pp. 84 - 85
U.S. Army Museum of Hawai'i (p. 84)
Courtesy Jay Otani (p. 85, inset)
Bishop Museum/United Japanese Society (p. 85, right)

Pp. 86 - 87
Courtesy Nancy Hedemann, Robert Huber Collection
    (p. 86, inset)
Costa Collection (p. 87, all three images)

Pp. 92 - 93
Honolulu Theatre for Youth/Nieva Photo (image 1)
Honolulu Academy of Arts (image 2)
Olivier Koning (image 3)
Diamond Head Theatre, Camera Hawai'i Photo
    (image 4)
Honolulu Symphony, Camera Hawai'i/Werner Stoy
    Photo (image 5)
Costa Collection (images 6, 7 - Honolulu Community
    Theatre)

Pp. 94 - 95
Mazeppa Costa (images 2, 3)
IHP (images 4, 7)
The Kamehameha Schools/De Ponte Photo (image 5)
Costa Collection, Tradewinds Records (image 6)

P. 97
Costa Collection (inset)

P. 98
Costa Collection (right)

Pp. 104 - 105
The Honolulu Advertiser/Monte Costa (image 2)
©Monte Costa (image 3)
Costa Collection (images 4, 7, 8-R - Wiley Photo)
Mazeppa Costa (images 5, 6, 10)
Courtesy Governor's Office, State of Hawai'i (image 9)

Pp. 106 - 107
WATG Architects/R. Wenkam Photo (image 1)
Courtesy Jay Otani (image 2)
WATG Architects Graphic Pictures Hawai'i (image 8)
Costa Collection (image 3 - *Beacon Magazine*; 4 - Herbert Bauer
    Photo; 5 - *Beacon Magazine*/Photo Hawai'i)
IHP (image 6)
Mazeppa Costa for WATG Architects (image 7)
Olivier Koning for WATG Architects (image 9)

Pp. 108 - 109
Mazeppa Costa (images 1, 2, 3, 4, 5, 7)
The Honolulu Advertiser, Monte Costa Photo (image 6)

Pp. 110 - 111; 112 - 113; 114 - 115
©Monte Costa

Endnotes

Chapter 1

1 Samuel Manaiaka'alani Kamakau, *The Works of the People of Old: No Ahana a ka Po'e Kahiko* (Honolulu: Bishop Museum Press, 1976), p. 59.
2 Tommy Holmes, *The Hawaiian Canoe* (Honolulu: Editions Limited, 1981), p. 109.
3 Ibid.
4 Te Rangi Hiroa (Peter H. Buck), *Arts and Crafts of Hawai'i VII, Fishing* (Honolulu: Bishop Museum Press, 1964), p. 286.
5 Holmes, pp. 109, 111.
6 Kamakau, pp. 61–64.
7 Kamakau, pp. 47–50.
8 Donald D. Kilolani Mitchell, *Resource Units in Hawaiian Culture* (Honolulu: The Kamehameha Schools Press, 1982), p. 152.
9 http://www.spiritofaloha.com/place (Carol Silva, "The Secret of Fire," *Spirit of Aloha* [July 1999].)
10 Holmes, pp. 109, 55.
11 Mitchell, p. 148.
12 Lynn J. Martin, *Traditions We Share* (Honolulu: State Foundation on Culture and the Arts, Honolulu Academy of Arts, 1997), p. 37.

Chapter 2

1 Albert F. Judd II, "Introduction, From the 1937 Edition," *Missionary Album: Sesquicentennial Edition 1820–1970*, Bernice Judd, advisor, and committee (Honolulu: Hawaiian Mission Children's Society, 1969), p. 3.
2 Additional sources for the Obookiah material:
Mary Cooke, *To Raise a Nation* (Kingsport, T.N.: Hawaiian Mission Children's Society, 1970), pp. 25–31.
Ralph S. Kuykendall and A. Grove Day, *Hawai'i: A History* (Englewood Cliffs, N.J.: Prentice Hall, Inc., 1948).
3 William Ellis, *Journal of William Ellis: A Narrative of a Tour Through Hawai'i in 1823* (Honolulu: Hawaiian Gazette Co., Ltd., 1917; reprint of the London 1827 edition).
4 Adrienne L. Kaeppler, *Polynesian Dance* (Honolulu: Alpha Delta Kappa Hawai'i, 1983), p. 18.
5 Mazeppa King Costa, "Dance in the Society and Hawaiian Islands, as presented by the Early Writers, 1767–1842," M.A. thesis, University of Hawai'i, 1951, pp. 96–97.
6 Ibid., pp. 97–98.
7 Jerry Hopkins, *The Hula* (Apa Productions [HK] Ltd.: 1982), p. 17.
8 Kaeppler, pp. 18–25.
9 Kaeppler, p. 24.